THINKING LIKE A CHRISTIAN

THINKING LIKE A CHRISTIAN

*Understanding and Living
a Biblical Worldview*

DAVID NOEBEL

WITH CHUCK EDWARDS

BROADMAN
&HOLMAN
PUBLISHERS

Nashville, Tennessee

Copyright © 2002 by David Noebel

Published in 2002 by Broadman & Holman Publishers
Nashville, Tennessee

DEWEY: 248.48
SUBHD: CHRISTIAN LIFE / DISCIPLESHIP

Unless otherwise noted, Scripture quotations have been taken from the Holman Christian Standard Bible®, copyright © 1999, 2000 by Holman Bible Publishers. Used by permission.

Cover and interior design by
The Gregory Group and Paul T. Gant, Art & Design—Nashville, TN

10-Digit ISBN: 0-8054-3895-5
13-Digit ISBN: 978-0-8054-3895-6

4 5 6 7 8 9   10 09 08 07 06 05

TABLE OF CONTENTS

Introduction to the
Thinking Like a Christian Study

HOW TO USE THIS TEXT

The *Thinking Like a Christian* study consists of four components which can be used independently or—for the best learning experience—in a coordinated teaching plan. The components are:

(1) This textbook
(2) A Leader's Guide CD included with this textbook
(3) A separate Student Journal for directed, interactive learning
(4) A separate Video that gives a comprehensive overview of biblical worldview thinking.

TO USE THIS TEXT AS AN INDEPENDENT RESOURCE

Getting a quick overview of this material will help you take in all it has to offer. To begin with, read the entire first chapter. Chapter 1 points out the significance of understanding Christianity from a worldview perspective. Then read the "Summary" sections at the beginnings of chapters 2–11. This will present the scope of our study. Following your review of the summaries, read Chapter 12 in its entirety. This chapter explains other worldviews that vie for attention (and devotion)—Secular Humanism, Marxism/Leninism, and Cosmic Humanism. While this text focuses on the Christian worldview, it is important to recognize the opposition to Christianity of other views and the individual and collective influence of those views on the world in which we live. Finally, read chapters 2–11 all the way through.

TO USE THIS TEXT IN CONJUNCTION WITH ONE OR MORE OF THE OTHER STUDY COMPONENTS

The above-mentioned method of reading the text works well as a start for using the larger *Thinking Like a Christian* study, and here is a summary of how each of the other elements contributes:

(1) **STUDENT JOURNAL.** The Student Journal expands the study of the world-view disciplines presented in each chapter of the text. The five daily exercises contain excerpts from corresponding chapters in the textbook. The Journal, however, is peppered with illustrations different from those found in the text, to give students a broader perspective on each week's topic. The pacing—one lesson for each of five school days per week—is designed to help students absorb the sometimes weighty concepts inherent in understanding a comprehensive worldview.

(2) **THE VIDEO.** The 60-minute, documentary-style video greatly enhances the learning process. It is divided into segments of approximately five minutes each, summarizing the ten disciplines. We recommend either of two viewing patterns:

> #1: WEEKLY LESSON REVIEW: View one 5-minute video segment on Friday of the week as a review of that week's lesson.

> #2: MID-TERM AND END-OF-COURSE REVIEW: Schedule two separate days for interactive discussion of the previous six lessons. You can stop the video after each 5-minute segment for a brief discussion, or students can simply watch the video and take notes as a review of the material.

(3) **THE CD LEADER'S GUIDE.** A forty-five minute interactive lesson introduces students to the topic for each week and is designed to foster interest in the subject studied. Each discipline is covered by a detailed lesson plan to simplify preparation, along with resources such as creative activities, worksheets, and handouts (permission is granted to reproduce them for the members of your class), and teaching outlines formatted to allow you to adapt lessons to your own knowledge level or teaching style.

PREFACE
JOSH McDOWELL

Speaker and author of best-sellers
Right from Wrong, Why Wait? and *Evidence that Demands a Verdict*

This generation is faced with the greatest and most serious cultural crisis in history. And the crisis is a direct result of a radical change in the way people view what is true.

I've given more than 23,000 talks to students in universities and high schools in 100 countries around the world. What I'm finding is this: When I make a statement about the deity of Christ, the resurrection, or the reliability of Scripture, I have people come up to me and say, *"What right do you have to say that? You're being intolerant! What right do you have to judge anyone's moral life?"*

These questions come from a totally different view of life than was once the case. We are now living in not just a post-Christian culture, but an anti-Christian culture!

That's why you face a challenge unlike any other in recent history. Before you can know how to respond to our changing culture, you must first understand how the Bible relates to all of life.

In this book, you will encounter a biblical worldview. Each chapter explains a way of looking at the world that gives hope, meaning and a greater understanding of how God fits into every part of your life. Once you've made this way of thinking your own, like the leaders from the small tribe of Issachar in the Old Testament, you will understand the times and know what you should do (1 Chronicles 12:32).

Josh

CHAPTER 1

Thinking about Worldviews

KEY QUESTION

What is a worldview?

KEY IDEA

A worldview is any ideology, philosophy, theology, movement, or religion that provides an overarching approach to understanding God, the world, and the relationship of people to God and the world.

KEY QUOTE

"I now believe that the balance of reasoned considerations tells heavily in favour of the religious, even of the Christian view of the world."

—C.E.M. Joad

SUMMARY

Every individual bases his or her thoughts, decisions and actions on a worldview. A person may not be able to identify this worldview, and it may lack consistency, but the most basic assumptions about the origin of life, purpose, and the future guarantee adherence to some system of thought.

Because worldviews are pertinent to every person's life—the way we think and the way we act—and because virtually all worldviews promise some sort of salvation or utopia, the study of worldviews is of critical importance.

This study lays out a biblical Christian worldview. The reason this approach is so crucial is that Christians today generally are not taught the importance of thinking in biblical categories. As a result, the Christian community is having little influence in the larger society, especially in the areas of education, government, and the mass media. And more tragically, we are losing our Christian young people to alien worldviews that dominate popular culture and the college campus.

By the time you complete this study, you should understand how certain ideas comprise a worldview's content and give it form. Christians will fight the good fight of faith, finish the course, and keep the faith (2 Timothy 4:7) if they understand the truth of their worldview.

After years of skepticism and relativism at work in America and abroad, the world yearns for a revival of soul and spirit—that is, a revival of truth. The biblical Christian worldview forms the basis for such a revival. This text sets forth that worldview.

Ask the average person about his or her philosophy of life and you will probably get some sort of answer, even if it turns out to be a little sketchy. While many people may not be sure what they believe, all admit to some set of ultimate beliefs and values. This set of beliefs is the basis for one's whole approach to life, or worldview. And while everyone has a worldview, most have a tough time defending what they hold to be true.

The reason it is difficult to discuss the issue of worldview is because our generation has lost the art of thinking deeply about why we believe what we believe. We are not accustomed to considering seriously life's most foundational questions. Yet, because actions are based on beliefs, everyone must start with a few basic assumptions about our place in the world. So the question is: "What's your worldview?" To answer that question we must define what is meant by the term "worldview."

How should a worldview be defined? This question has various answers depending on whom you read. Some Christians divide worldview along theological lines. Thus, worldview categories are listed as atheism (no God), theism (God is), pantheism (God is all), panentheism (God is in all), deism (God is transcendent), finite Godism (God is finite), and polytheism (God is many).

Every worldview attempts to answer questions about creation, the fundamental problems of the world, and the solution to those problems.

This is the approach of Norman Geisler in his book, *Worlds Apart.*

James Sire slices the worldview pie differently. In *The Universe Next Door,* Sire includes chapters on deism, naturalism, Christian theism, nihilism, existentialism, Eastern pantheistic monism, and the New Age. Then there is the approach of R.C. Sproul in *Lifeviews,* where he outlines secularism, pessimistic existentialism, sentimental humanism, pragmatism, positivism, pluralism, relativism, and hedonism. Using biblical terminology in his book, *How Now Shall We Live?*, Chuck Colson describes how every worldview answers three major questions: Where did we come from? (the question of creation), What's wrong with the world? (or what Christians call "the fall"), and What's the solution to man's basic problem? (the biblical term is "redemption").

UNDERSTANDING THE TIMES

While each of these approaches to worldview thinking is helpful in various ways, this text follows the divisions found in *Understanding the Times*.[1] In that book, David Noebel defines worldview by using the following ten disciplines: theology, philosophy, biology, psychology, ethics, sociology, law, politics, economics, and history. This arrangement has several advantages. First, as will be discussed in more detail later in this chapter, each of these disciplines is a part of God's creative and redemptive order. They are not artificially derived constructs, but are actually a reflection of how God made the world, ordered man's place in it, and redeemed it.

> *"A worldview is a way of viewing or interpreting all of reality. It is an interpretive framework through which or by which one makes sense of the data of life and the world."*[2]
>
> —Norman Geisler, William Watkins

Second, these ten categories are easy for the average student to identify. At some point in life, everyone asks the question, "What about God?" (theology). Also, we are curious about what is real and how we know what is true (the questions philosophy ponders). We have questions about life's origins (biology), how to understand

EVERY DISCIPLINE EXAMINES ITS OWN WORLDVIEW QUESTION	
Discipline	**Question**
Theology	Is there a God, and what is God like?
Philosophy	What is real, and what is true?
Biology	What is the origin of life?
Psychology	What is the basic nature of mankind?
Ethics	What is right?
Sociology	How should society be structured?
Law	What is the basis for law?
Politics	What is the purpose of government?
Economics	What produces a sound economy?
History	How should we interpret human events?

ourselves (psychology) and what makes choices right or wrong (the study of ethics). We wonder about how society ought to be structured (sociology), how to solve legal issues (law), what our system of government should look like (politics), how we ought to make, save, spend, and give money (economics), and how our lives are affected by the past (history).

Each of these areas is relevant to every one of us. Our educational enterprise is structured around these disciplines, with universities offering courses in each discipline to seek out answers to these vital questions. Dividing a worldview into these ten disciplines corresponds with how we approach life's important questions.

"All branches of knowledge are connected together, because the subject matter of knowledge is intimately united in itself, as being the acts and the work of the Creator." [3]

—JOHN H. NEWMAN

Third, dividing a worldview this way helps the student see connections between the various disciplines. It demonstrates how a worldview is built upon the foundational studies of theology and philosophy. Visualize a fruit tree with these two categories forming the root system. All the other categories are the fruit of what one thinks about God (theology) and reality (philosophy). Pictured this way, a worldview is a coherent, organic whole, with the fruit (outward behavior) flowing naturally from the root (inner beliefs). This unifying aspect of worldview thinking will become more apparent as you move through this text and corresponding course of study.

Finally, slicing a worldview into these major disciplines allows for easy comparison between competing worldviews, such as Secular Humanism, Marxism-Leninism, and Cosmic Humanism (comprising both New Age pantheism and neo-paganism, i.e., Wicca.) While our primary concern in this text is to develop a biblical Christian worldview, we will occasionally mention these other views by way of contrast to highlight specific issues. For a brief overview of Secular Humanism, Marxism-Leninism, and Cosmic Humanism, see Chapter 12 along with the summaries found in the chart in Appendix A.

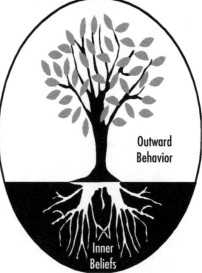

THE HEART OF A WORLDVIEW

The term "worldview" refers to any ideology, philosophy, theology, movement, or religion that provides an overarching approach to understanding God, the world, and man's relationship to God and the world. Specifically, a worldview should provide a particular perspective on each of the following ten disciplines: theology, philosophy, biology, psychology, ethics, sociology, law, politics, economics, and history. These disciplines also have implications for cultural expression such as found in the visual and performing arts, music, and literature.[4] Since biblical Christianity offers a specific stance or attitude toward all ten disciplines, it is, by our definition, a worldview.

A worldview also offers a particular perspective from which to approach each discipline. Conversely, each discipline is laden with values that have worldview implications. Christians must understand that these various disciplines are not value-free. Each discipline demands basic assumptions about the nature of reality in order to grant meaning to specific approaches to it.

This text analyzes how the Bible portrays a total worldview related to each of the ten disciplines. We are attempting to understand each discipline and how it fits into an overall picture of reality. No discipline stands alone. Each affects all others in one way or another. The line separating theology and philosophy is fragile; the line separating theology, philosophy, ethics, law, and politics is more so. In fact, there is no ultimate line, only a difference in emphasis and perspective.

> In the end, all ten disciplines form one piece of cloth.

Thus, the arrangement of the categories is, to some degree, arbitrary, but we have tried to place them in their most logical sequence. It is clear that theological and philosophical assumptions color every aspect of one's worldview and that disciplines such as sociology and psychology are related, but other relations and distinctions are less recognizable. Therefore, one reader may feel that we have inappropriately distanced law from ethics, and another may feel history to be almost as foundational to a worldview as philosophy. Our format is a logical suggestion; it is not binding. Besides, in the end, all ten disciplines form one piece of cloth.

A BIBLICAL CHRISTIAN WORLDVIEW	
SUBJECT	**VIEWPOINT**
THEOLOGY	View of God: Theism
PHILOSOPHY	View of Reality: Supernaturalism
BIOLOGY	View of Origin: Creation
PSYCHOLOGY	View of Mankind: Fallen Human Nature
ETHICS	View of Morality: Ethical Absolutes
SOCIOLOGY	View of Social Institutions: Traditional Home, Church and State
LAW	View of Source of Law: Natural Law
POLITICS	View of Government's Role: Justice/Freedom/Order
ECONOMICS	View of Economy: Stewardship of Property
HISTORY	View of Meaning in History: Historical Resurrection

A BIBLICAL CHRISTIAN WORLDVIEW

This text will demonstrate how Christianity provides a consistent explanation of all the facts of reality with regard to theology, philosophy, ethics, economics, or anything else. As Carl F.H. Henry says, "The Christian belief system, which the Christian knows to be grounded in divine revelation, is relevant to all of life."[5] This relevance results from the fact that Christianity is the one worldview based on truth. "Christianity is true," says George Gilder, "and its truth will be discovered anywhere you look very far."[6] Gilder, who is not only an outstanding economic philosopher but also a sociologist, found Christ while seeking sociological truth.

Philosopher C.E.M. Joad found Christ and Christianity because he was seeking ethical truth. "I now believe," he wrote, "that the balance of reasoned considerations tells heavily in favour of the religious, even of the Christian view of the world."[7] Joad recognized the need for absolute truth, rather than a truth that evolves with each new theory: "A religion which is in constant process of revision to square with science's ever-changing picture of the world might well be easier to believe, but it is hard to believe it would be worth believing."[8]

Christianity is the embodiment of Christ's claim

> *"Christianity is true, and its truth will be discovered anywhere you look very far."*
> —GEORGE GILDER

that he is "the way, the truth, and the life" (John 14:6). When we say "this is the Christian way," we mean "this is the way Christ would have us act in such a situation." It is no small matter to think and act as Christ instructs. Therefore, Christians agree with humanist Bertrand Russell's admission that "What the world needs is Christian love or compassion."[9]

America is often described as a Christian nation. Over 150 years ago, Alexis de Tocqueville wrote, "There is no country in the whole world, in which the Christian religion retains a greater influence over the souls of men than in America;

> *"There is no country in the whole world, in which the Christian religion retains a greater influence over the souls of men than in America."*
>
> —ALEXIS DE TOCQUEVILLE

and there can be no greater proof of its utility, and of its conformity to human nature, than that its influence is most powerfully felt over the most enlightened and free nation of the earth."[10] Unfortunately, however, America—and the rest of Western Civilization—are turning away from their heritage. Western nations are eradicating large chunks of Christianity from the public square.

> *"Truth will ultimately prevail where there is pains taken to bring it to light."*
>
> —GEORGE WASHINGTON

We contend that America should be moving in the opposite direction—embracing the Christian worldview rather than pushing it away. Francis Schaeffer blames America's drift toward secularism and injustice on the Christian community's failure to apply its worldview to every facet of society: "The basic problem of the Christians in this country in the last eighty years or so, in regard to society and in regard to government, is that they have seen things in bits and pieces instead of totals."[11] He goes on to say that

Pursuing consumerism and entertainment, many people now see life in bits and pieces rather than as a meaningful whole.

Christians have very gradually "become disturbed over permissiveness, pornography, the public schools, the breakdown of the family, and finally abortion. But they have not seen this as a totality—each thing being a part, a symptom of a much larger problem. They have failed to see that all of this has come about due to a shift in the worldview—that is, through a fundamental change in the overall way people think and view the world and life as a whole."[12]

1 Chronicles 12:32
From the Issacharites, who understood the times and knew what Israel should do: 200 chiefs with all their kinsmen under their command.

This study is a wake-up call for Christians living in America. A country seeking to promote human rights and religious, political, and economic liberty must adhere to the only worldview that can account for the existence of those concepts. Unfortunately, countless Americans are embracing other worldviews.

This, then, is our fundamental reason for preparing this text and the accompanying study guide: too many Christian young people are ill-prepared to lead. The vast majority have no concept of the components of their worldview and stand intellectually naked before left-wing university professors and the liberal media. Henry says that evangelical students know more about God than their secular counterparts, but "with some few gratifying exceptions, neither home nor church has shaped a comprehensive and consistent faith that stands noon-bright amid the dim shadows of spiritual rebellion and moral profligacy."[13] Christ's teachings impart just such a noon-bright faith to all Christians who master their worldview, who "understand the times." This book's foundational verse, 1 Chronicles 12:32, announces that just two hundred individuals who "understood the

Many young people are poorly prepared to face the challenges that contemporary college studies present to a Christian worldview.

times" provided the leadership for an entire nation. We believe that a comprehensive knowledge of a Christian worldview will provide today's young people with the understanding necessary to become Christian leaders and defenders of the faith once delivered to the saints by the apostles and prophets (Jude 3).

> *Jude 3*
> *Dear friends, although I was eager to write you about our common salvation, I found it necessary to write and exhort you to contend for the faith that was delivered to the saints once for all.*

THE SECULAR AND THE SACRED

Many people believe that when Christians confront other worldviews and attempt to speak to such "secular" disciplines as politics, economics, biology, and law, they are overstepping their bounds. "Mind your own business," we are told. Jesus taught His followers, "you are not of the world, but I have chosen you out of the world" (John 15:19).

> *"I believe Christianity is the only logical, consistent faith in the world."*
> —MORTIMER ADLER

How, then, can the Christian justify his claim to a worldview that speaks to every facet of life? Shouldn't he stick to spiritual matters and allow non-Christians to concentrate on the practical matters of running the world?

In short, isn't there a difference between the secular and the sacred?

Not according to Dietrich Bonhoeffer, who says we should not distinguish between the two: "There are not two realities, but only one reality, and that is the reality of God, which has become manifest in Christ in the reality of the world." [14] From the biblical Christian perspective, the ten disciplines addressed in this text reflect various aspects of God's creative and redemptive order. God created mankind with theological, philosophical, biological, ethical, etc., dimensions. We live and move and have our being (our very essence and existence) within and about these categories. Why? Because that is the way God created us.

Such being the case, these categories are, from the Christian perspective, sacred and not secular. They are sacred because they are imprinted in the creative order. Both the early record of Genesis and the life of Jesus Christ reflect this truth.

GOD'S CREATIVE AND REDEMPTIVE ORDERS

All ten disciplines are addressed in just the first few chapters of the Bible because they manifest and accent certain aspects of the creative order. For example:

- Genesis 1:1—"In the beginning God created the heavens and the earth"—is value-laden with theological and philosophical ramifications.
- Genesis 2:9—"the knowledge of good and evil"—contains ethical ramifications;
- Genesis 1:21—"according to their kinds"—biological;
- Genesis 2:7—"the man became a living being"—psychological;
- Genesis 1:28—"be fruitful, and multiply, fill the earth"—sociological and ecological;
- Genesis 3:11—"I had forbidden you"—legal;
- Genesis 9:6—"Whoever sheds man's blood"—political and legal;
- Genesis 1:29—"This will be food for you"—economic;
- Genesis 10:1—"These are the family records of Noah's sons: Shem, Ham, and Japheth…"—historical.

> 2 Corinthians 10:4–5
> We demolish arguments and every high-minded thing that is raised up against the knowledge of God, taking every thought captive to the obedience of Christ.

Further, God manifests Himself in the form of Christ in such a way as to underline the significance of each discipline:

- In theology, Jesus Christ is "the entire fullness of God's nature" (Colossians 2:9);
- In philosophy, Christ is the logos of God (John 1:1);
- In ethics, Christ is "the true light" (John 1:9, 3:19-20);
- In biology, Christ is "that life" (John 1:4, 11:25; Colossians 1:16);
- In psychology, Christ is "Savior" (Luke 1:46-47; Titus 2:13);
- In sociology, Christ is "Son" (Luke 1:30-31; Isaiah 9:6);
- In law, Christ is lawgiver (Genesis 49:10; Isaiah 9:7);
- In politics, Christ is "King of kings and Lord of lords" (Revelation 19:16; 1 Timothy 6:15; Isaiah 9:6; Luke 1:33);
- In economics, Christ is Owner of all things (Psalm 24:1; 50:10-12; 1 Corinthians 10:26);
- In history, Christ is "the Alpha and the Omega" (Revelation 1:8).

The integration of these various categories into society has come to be known as Western Civilization. For an overview of God's Creative and Redemptive Order, see the chart in Appendix B.

The Bible and the life of Jesus Christ provide the Christian with the basis for a complete worldview. Indeed, Christians gain a perspective so comprehensive that they are commanded to be "taking every thought captive to the obedience of Christ" (2 Corinthians 10:5).

> *"Faith is the central problem of this age."*
> —WHITTAKER CHAMBERS

Once we have captured all thoughts and made them obedient to Christ, we are to use these thoughts to "demolish arguments and every high-minded thing that is raised up against the knowledge of God" (2 Corinthians 10:4-5). When nations and men forget God (see Psalm 2) they experience what mankind has experienced in the twentieth century. Nazism and communism, two major movements bereft of the knowledge of God, cost the human race tens of millions of lives. Whittaker Chambers says that communism's problem is not a problem of economics, but of atheism: "Faith is the central problem of this age."[15] Alexander Solzhenitsyn echoes him: "Men have forgotten God."[16]

The Apostle Paul insists in Colossians 2 that those who have "received Christ Jesus the Lord" (Colossians 2:6) are to be rooted and built up in him, strengthened in the faith as they were taught (Colossians 2:7). While the Christian works to strengthen his faith or worldview, he must see to it that no one takes him "captive through philosophy and empty deceit based on human tradition, based on the elemental forces of the world, and not based on Christ" (Colossians 2:8). From the

> *"Men have forgotten God."*
> —ALEXANDER SOLZHENITSYN

Christian point of view Secular, Marxist, and Cosmic Humanism fall within the realm of "the elemental forces of the world." They are based on the wisdom of this world and not upon Christ.

This wasn't merely a point of doctrine for Paul. He practiced what he preached. In Acts 17, Paul confronted the vain and deceitful philosophies of the atheistic Epicureans and pantheistic Stoics—the professional humanists of his day. The Apostle countered their ideas with Christian ideas; he reasoned and preached, and he accented three Christian truths—the resurrection of Jesus Christ (Acts 17:18), the creation of the universe by God (Acts 17:24), and the judgment to come (Acts 17:31).

Can we do less? We, too, must fearlessly proclaim the good news of the gospel (God created the universe and all things in it; mankind rebelliously smashed the image of God by sin; Jesus Christ died for our sin, was raised from the dead, and is alive forevermore [1 Corinthians 15:1-4]), and we must stand fast in the context of the same worldview as Paul— creation, resurrection, and judgment.

> **Certain non-Christian worldviews are religious.**

Paul recognized that people dare not compartmentalize life into boxes marked "sacred" and "secular." He understood not only that Christianity was both a worldview and a religion, but also that all worldviews are religious by definition. Indeed, he went so far as to tell the Epicureans and Stoics that they were religious —they just worshiped an "Unknown God."

Most people have no problem recognizing that certain non-Christian worldviews are religious. Cosmic Humanists talk about god, so they must practice a religion. But how can the "religious" label apply to atheists like the Marxists or Secular Humanists?

It applies because all worldviews include a theology. That is, all begin with a religious declaration:

- Christianity begins with "In the beginning God."
- Marxism/Leninism and Secular Humanism begin with "In the beginning no God."
- Cosmic Humanism begins with the declaration "Everything is God."

> Both Secular Humanism and Marxism are religious worldviews.

Christians who have seen their worldview effectively eliminated from the public schools are rightfully outraged by the humanists' violations of the present interpretation of the First Amendment. They are angered that a mere 7.3 million humanists can control the content of American public schooling while the country's Christians provide the lion's share of the students and bear the majority of the cost through their tax dollars.

Humanists attempt to downplay their violation of the present interpretation of the First Amendment by claiming that they present a neutral viewpoint. But no educational approach is neutral, as Richard A. Baer notes: "Education never takes place in a moral and philosophical vacuum.

> Trying to separate the sacred from the secular is like trying to sever the soul from the body.

If the larger questions about human beings and their destiny are not being asked and answered within a predominantly Judeo-Christian framework [worldview], they will be addressed with another philosophical or religious framework—but hardly one that is 'neutral.'"[17]

Clearly, both Secular Humanism and Marxism are religious worldviews. Trying to separate the sacred from the secular is like trying to sever the soul from the body—a deadly experiment. Thus, in order to provide a fair educational system for our young people, we must recognize that all worldviews have religious implications and that it is discriminatory to bar some worldviews and not others from the classroom.

A WORD ABOUT SOURCES

The Bible, of course, is the primary source for the Christian worldview. Christianity explains the facts of reality better than any other worldview because it relies upon divine inspiration. If the Bible is truly God's special revelation to man, as we believe it is, then the only completely accurate view of the world must be founded on Scripture.

The divine inspiration of Scripture explains not only its miraculous coherency but also the incredible power of the figure of Christ. Atheist historian W.E.H. Lecky admits that the character of Jesus "has been not only the highest pattern of virtue but the strongest incentive to its practice; and has exercised so deep an influence that it may be truly said that the simple record of three short years of active life has done more to regenerate and to soften mankind than all the disquisitions of philoso-

Because God's special revelation is presented in the Bible, an accurate worldview must be founded on Scripture.

phers, and all the exhortations of moralists."[18] We believe the reason for this is that when Christ told the woman who spoke of the Messiah, "I am He, the One speaking to you" (John 4:26), He was telling her the most fundamental truth of all. What Christ said concerning life and death, the saved and lost condition of mankind, body and soul, and truth encompasses the central precepts of the Christian worldview. Christ is its cornerstone. He is the way, the truth, and the life (John 14:6).

> The Christian worldview stands or falls on the accuracy of the Bible.

When presenting the Christian worldview, then, we take the Bible at face value. Call it "literal" interpretation if you wish, but it is difficult to see how else the writers of the Old and New Testaments meant to be taken. Figures of speech—yes, typologies—yes, analogies—yes, but overall they wrote in simple, straightforward terms. When a writer says, "In the beginning God created the heavens and the earth," we understand him to say that there is a God, there was a beginning to creation, that heaven and earth exist, and that God made them.

It does not take a Ph.D. or a high IQ to comprehend the basic message of the Bible. God's special revelation is open to everyone. There is no room for an "intellectual elite" in Christianity; only one "high priest" need intercede between God and man—Jesus Christ. For this reason, every man may "approach the throne of grace with boldness" (Hebrews 4:14-16).

This text also will rely on Christian men and women to describe the Christian worldview. "If we accept the testimony of men, God's testimony is greater, because it is God's testimony that He has given about His Son." (1 John 5:9). The Christian worldview stands or falls on the accuracy of the Bible.

British writer and philosopher C.S. Lewis offered a concise picture of the Christian worldview in his classic book *Mere Christianity.*

STUDY PROCEDURES

This work paints the various categorical positions with broad strokes, adhering to Albert Einstein's dictum: Everything should be made as simple as possible, but not simpler. Each chapter, we know, could consume thousands of pages by itself. Millions of pages and billions of words have been written on Christian theism alone. We have attempted, therefore, not to address every subtlety of each approach, but rather to capture the kernel of each discipline. We follow C.S. Lewis' formula, striving to capture "mere Christianity." Thus, we examine the core, the foundational approach, of each discipline. In this way, we assure the reader a text that will never become outdated.

If you are interested in additional study about worldview, you would do well to read James Orr's *A Christian View of God and the World,* along with *A Christian Manifesto* by Francis Schaeffer and Chuck Colson's *How Now Shall We Live?.* These works make a fitting addition to this study by helping you think in terms of worldviews and enforcing the notion that ideas have consequences—even logical consequences that proceed from prior beliefs.

RECOMMENDED READING FOR ADVANCED STUDY: APOLOGETICS

Bauman, Michael, David Hall, and Robert Newman. *Evangelical Apologetics.* Camp Hill, Pa.: Christian Publications, 1996.

Craig, William Lane. *Reasonable Faith: Christian Truth and Apologetics* Wheaton, Ill.: Crossway Books, 1994.

Geisler, Norman L. *Christian Apologetics.* Grand Rapids, Mich.: Baker Book House, 1988.

McDowell, Josh. *The New Evidence that Demands a Verdict.* Nashville: Thomas Nelson, 1999.

RECOMMENDED READING FOR ADVANCED STUDY: GENERAL WORLDVIEW STUDIES

Breese, David. *Seven Men that Rule the World from the Grave.* Chicago: Moody Press, 1993.

Colson, Charles. *Kingdoms in Conflict.* Grand Rapids, Mich.: Zondervan, 1989.

Colson, Charles and Nancy Pearcey. *How Now Shall We Live?* Wheaton, Ill.: Tyndale House, 1999.

LaHaye, Tim, and David Noebel. *Mind Siege: The Battle for Truth in the New Millennium.* Nashville: Word Publishing, 2000.

Nash, Ronald H. *Worldviews in Conflict.* Grand Rapids, Mich.: Zondervan, 1992.

Noebel, David A. *Understanding the Times: The Religious Worldviews of Our Day and the Search for Truth.* Eugene, Ore.: Harvest House, 1991.

Noebel, David A., J. F. Baldwin, and Kevin J. Bywater. *Clergy in the Classroom: The Religion of Secular Humanism,* 2nd edition, Manitou Springs, Col.: Summit Press, 2001.

Schaeffer, Francis A. *How Should We Then Live?.* Wheaton, Ill.: Crossway Books, 1983.

Veith, Gene Edward, Jr. *Postmodern Times: A Christian Guide to Contemporary Thought and Culture.* Wheaton, Ill.: Crossway Books, 1994.

ENDNOTES

1. See David A. Noebel, *Understanding the Times* (Eugene, Ore.: Harvest House, 1991).

2. Norman L. Geisler and William D. Watkins, *Worlds Apart* (Baker Book House, Grand Rapids, 1989), p. 11.

3. Quoted in David A. Noebel, *Understanding the Times* (Eugene, Ore.: Harvest House, 1991) p. 9.

4. Some may ask where the arts (the visual and performing arts, literature, music, and film) come into a worldview. There are two options: you could either have an eleventh category for "The Arts," or this area can be subsumed under "Sociology," as a means of outwardly expressing our worldview in a cultural way. This course of study does not specifically focus on the arts, although we use examples from movies and music to illustrate the worldviews being presented. For more information on a Christian approach to the arts, see Francis Schaeffer's landmark book, *How Shall We Then Live?* Other more recent works include Neil Postman's *Amusing Ourselves to Death: Public Discourse in the Age of Show Business*, Steve Turner's *Imagine: A Vision for Christians in the Arts*, Gene Veith's *State of the Arts: From Bezalel to Mapplethorpe*, H. R. Rookmaaker's *Modern Art and the Death of Culture*, Kenneth Myers' *All God's Children and Blue Suede Shoes: Christians & Popular Culture*, and Carson Holloway's *All Shook Up: Music, Passion, and Politics*. Or you might consider David Quine's "Adventures in Art," a curriculum designed for home use found on his website at: www.cornerstonecurriculum.com/Curriculum_art.htm

5. Carl F.H. Henry, *Toward a Recovery of Christian Belief* (Westchester, Ill.: Crossway Books, 1990), p. 113.

6. L. Neff, "*Christianity Today* Talks to George Gilder," *Christianity Today*, March 6, 1987, p. 35.

7. C.E.M. Joad, *The Recovery of Belief* (London: Faber and Faber, 1955), p. 22.

8. Ibid., p. 240.

9. Bertrand Russel, *Human Society in Ethics and Politics* (New York: Mentor, 1962), p. viii.

10. Alexis de Tocqueville, *Democracy in America,* two volumes (New Rochelle, N.Y.: Arlington House, n.d.), vol. 1, p. 294. Elsewhere he declared, "The Americans combine the notions of Christianity and of liberty so intimately in their minds, that it is impossible to make them conceive the one without the other" (p. 297).

11. Francis A. Schaeffer, *A Christian Manifesto* (Westchester, Ill.: Crossway Books, 1981), p. 17.

12. Ibid.

13. Carl F.H. Henry, *Twilight of a Great Civilization* (Westchester, Ill. Crossway Books, 1988), p. 94.

14. H. Burtness, "Bonhoeffer, Dietrich," in *Baker's Dictionary of Christian Ethics,* ed. Carl F.H. Henry, (Grand Rapids, Mich.: Baker, 1973), p. 67.

15. Whittaker Chambers, *Witness* (Lake Bluff, Ill.: Random House, 1952), p. 17.

16. Alexander Solzhenitsyn, Harvard Lectures.

17. Richard A. Baer, "They Are Teaching Religion in Public Schools," *Christianity Today*, February 17, 1984, p. 15.

18. W.E.H. Lecky, *History of European Morals (from Augustus to Charlemagne),* two volumes (New York: George Braziller, 1955), vol. 2, pp. 8-9.

CHAPTER 2

Theology

KEY QUESTION

Is there a God, and what is God like?

KEY IDEA

Christ's teachings and actions as revealed in the
Bible provide the cornerstone for special revelation
and a solid foundation for Christian theism.

KEY QUOTE

"Theism, the belief that God is, and atheism, the
belief that God is not, are not simply two beliefs.
They are two fundamental ways of seeing the
whole of existence. The one, theism, sees existence
as ultimately meaningful, as having a meaning
beyond itself; the other sees existence as having no
meaning beyond itself."[1]
—STEPHEN D. SCHWARZ

SUMMARY

The theology of Christianity is the affirmation of the existence of an intelligent, powerful, loving, just, and awesome God who exists in the Trinity of Father, Son, and Holy Spirit. From the Christian perspective, "In the beginning God" (Genesis 1:1) is the foundation for all meaning. Christianity further proclaims that this powerful, intelligent God who created all things in heaven and earth is the same God who took upon Himself human form in the person of Jesus Christ and died for our sins. Christianity proclaims a God who is both Mind and Heart—who not only created the world, but also loves it so much that He sent His only begotten Son to die for it. Christian theism declares in large letters, "God is," "God created," "God loves," and "God judges."

Christian theism rests primarily on two foundations: special revelation (the Bible) and general revelation (the created order). While the Bible reveals the character and personality of God page after page, the "whole workmanship of the universe," according to John Calvin, reveals and discloses God day after day.

James Orr explains that the theistic position is established not by any single clue or evidence, but by "the concurrent forces of many, starting from different and independent standpoints."[2] Christians see evidences of God everywhere. It is the Christian position that history, theology, philosophy, science, mathematics, logic, and experience all point to the existence of a Creator and Redeemer.

SPECIAL REVELATION

Christian theists believe that God has revealed Himself to mankind in a general way through creation and in a special (personal) way evidenced by His divine words and acts contained in the Bible and especially in the person of Jesus Christ. Millard Erickson defines the two forms of revelation this way: "On the one hand, general revelation is God's communication of Himself to all persons, at all times, and in all places. Special revelation on the other hand, involves God's particular communications and manifestations which are available now only by consultation of certain sacred writings."[3]

General revelation has been viewed throughout church history by

At 9,100 feet, Mt. Hermon is the highest mountain in Syria and is believed by some scholars to be the place where the transfiguration of Jesus—a divine revelation to His disciples—took place.

a variety of Christian theists as a necessary but insufficient means for providing knowledge about the Creator and His character. It is better theology and philosophy to begin with the God of the Bible to explain the universe than to begin with the universe to explain God.

According to the Christian view, the destiny of created mankind involves both salvation and judgment. It is not general revelation but special revelation—the Bible—that answers such questions as: How can mankind be saved? From what must mankind be saved? Why will judgment occur? Special revelation, then, is "special" because it is the key that opens the door to both heaven and earth.

The unified message of the biblical writers, despite the extreme diversity of their circumstances and backgrounds, argues for the divine inspiration of Scripture.

> **General revelation** refers to the means by which God reveals Himself to mankind through the physical universe and the moral order.

One of the most basic tenets of Christian belief is the divine inspiration of the Bible. When the individual accepts the Bible as the Word of God, the teachings and events it describes become the most important basis for understanding all reality. Without faith that the Bible is God's Word, people are left floundering—forced to trust their own (unfounded) thought processes as the ultimate criteria for discerning truth. No one can deny the Bible's divine inspiration and still claim to be a biblical Christian for the simple reason that Scripture proclaims itself to be God-breathed (2 Timothy 3:16-17). If one believes the Bible to be a true and accurate document, then one must accept its claim to be divinely inspired.

The evidence in support of the Christian's belief in the divine inspiration of the Bible is convincing. For example, the unity of teaching in the Bible is startling in light of the fact that its books were

> **One of the most basic tenets of Christian belief is the divine inspiration of the Bible.**

authored by different men faced with very different circumstances. Further, the astounding ability of the Bible to change the lives of individuals (for the better) who accept its authority strengthens its claim to be a special revelation from God. The degree of moral truth contained in the Bible also supports its divine inspiration. All these arguments support the belief that the Bible is God's Word; however, the most convincing witness for divine inspiration is the Bible itself. Those hesitant to

God's general revelation is evident through the obvious order in creation—from the structure of the universe to the arrangement of atoms.

accept Scripture as God's special revelation are most often convinced by a thorough, open-minded study of the Bible.

In studying the Bible, the reader meets God's most direct form of special revelation: the person of Jesus Christ. "In Jesus of Nazareth," writes Carl F.H. Henry, "the divine source of revelation and the divine content of that revelation converge and coincide."[4] Christ's teachings and actions as revealed in the Bible provide the cornerstone for special revelation and a solid foundation for Christian theism.

The purpose of divine revelation lies in its communication to the Christian of the significance of Christ's teachings and actions. The third member of the Trinity, the Holy Spirit, plays an important role in this dialogue. Henry explains: "Scripture itself is given so that the Holy Spirit may etch God's Word upon the hearts of his followers in ongoing sanctification that anticipates the believer's final, unerring conformity to the image of Jesus Christ, God's incarnate Word."[5] This is the ultimate reason God chose to reveal Himself and His plan for mankind in the Bible.

> **Special revelation** refers to the specific means by which God reveals Himself to mankind through the Bible and in the person of Jesus Christ.

For this reason, the Christian's reliance on the Bible should be profound and constantly renewed. Christians do not read the Bible once and set it aside. Rather, they study it as the Word of God and work constantly to conform to its teachings. Christians spend their lives seeking to understand the powerful message of the Bible.

> *"Unless I believe in God, I can't believe in thought; so I can never use thought to disbelieve in God."*
> —C.S. LEWIS

DESIGN AND GENERAL REVELATION

Special revelation, then, is the linchpin of Christianity, while general revelation serves as a prod to encourage man to recognize the ultimate truths set down in Scripture and embodied in Jesus Christ.

The majesty of nature, as well as our own thought processes, are evidences for God's existence, according to C.S. Lewis.

Although God's revelation through nature, in and of itself, fails to bring men to a saving knowledge of God, it is capable of bringing men to a general knowledge of God. A great majority of intellectuals agree that the concepts of purpose and design, for example, have validity in regard to the question of the existence of God.

Anglican clergyman William Paley argued in *Natural Theology* (a book about which Charles Darwin admitted, "I do not think I hardly ever admired a book more . . ."[6]) that a man chancing upon a watch in the wilderness could not conclude that the watch had simply always existed; rather, the obvious design of the watch—not only its internal makeup but also the fact that it clearly exists for a purpose—would necessarily imply the existence of its designer. Paley went on to substitute the universe for the watch and contended that a mechanism so obviously designed as the universe necessitated the existence of a grand Designer. This is an excellent example of the way in which the created order reveals the existence of God.

The universe forces its sense of design (and thus a Designer) on all men open to such a possibility. Many discover God through the general revelation of a structured universe; many others encounter Him in the purposeful nature of reality. C.E.M. Joad, who was an atheist for much of his professional career, wrote a book entitled *The Recovery of Belief* shortly before his death. This book traces his gradual advance toward God and Jesus Christ. Joad was largely convinced by his observation of human nature—that a moral law exists, and that men often flaunt that law.

Still another twist on the argument for the general revelation of God's existence is presented by C. S. Lewis. "Suppose there were no intelligence behind the universe," says Lewis. "In that case nobody designed my brain for the purpose of thinking. Thought is merely the by-product of some atoms within my skull. But if so, how can I trust my own thinking to be true?" asks Lewis. "But if I can't trust my own thinking, of course, I can't trust the arguments leading to atheism, and therefore have no reason to be an atheist, or anything else. Unless I believe in God, I can't believe in thought; so I can never use thought to disbelieve in God."[7] The evidence points to what Christians believe—that a personal God has revealed Himself through a created world, that He has a plan for that world, and an ultimate destiny for it.

WHAT DOES REVELATION TELL US ABOUT GOD?

The Christian is concerned not only with the existence of God in general, but also with the relationship that exists between God and man, and particularly with the redemption of all mankind. While Secular Humanists declare in the *Humanist Manifesto II* that no God can save us—"we must save ourselves"—Christian theism echoes Thomas, the disciple who referred to Jesus as "My Lord and My God" (John 20:28), and Peter, who said to Jesus, "You have the words of eternal life" (John 6:68). God, as revealed throughout the Bible and especially in the person of Christ, is clearly knowable and desires to be known.

To say that God is knowable is also to say that God "relates" or has personality—that

He is "personal." God's self-awareness, His emotions, and His self-determining will make up the core of His divine personality. The Bible is emphatic in describing

> *"I Am Who I Am."*
>
> EXODUS 3:14

God as a person aware of Himself. In Isaiah 44:6, God says, "I am the first and I am the last, and there is no God besides me." In Exodus 3:14, God says to Moses, "I Am Who I Am."

Besides possessing self-awareness, the God of the Bible (like man) has sensibilities. At times God is portrayed as sorrowful (Genesis 6:6), angry (Deuteronomy 1:37), compassionate (Psalm 111:4), jealous (Exodus 20:5), and able to show satisfaction (Genesis 1:4). Theologians do not feel that such scriptures suggest that God is limited, but rather that God is willing to reveal Himself in an anthropomorphic, personal way to people.

CHARACTERISTICS OF THE PERSONAL GOD

Besides believing that God is a personal God and communicates His nature, Christians believe that God is self-determining—that is, sovereign in regard to His will. God's self-determination is described in Daniel 4:35: "All the inhabitants of the earth are counted as nothing, and He does what He wants with the army of heaven and the inhabitants of the earth. There is no one who can hold back His hand or say to Him, 'What have You done?'"

In addition to being self-determining, the God of the Bible is moral. Proverbs 15:3 warns us that God distinguishes between good and evil and that He is concerned with our morality (see also Proverbs 5:21). God's uncompromisingly moral character is one of the most crucial aspects of His being. A true understanding of God's absolute goodness leads the individual unerringly to the conclusion that every man has an acute need for a Redeemer.

Long-suffering patience and faithfulness are also personality traits of God. God's willingness to delay His judgment upon the Israelites when they worshipped the golden calf (Exodus 32:11-14) and His faithful promise to save the believer from eternal judgment (John 10:28) are prime examples of His patience and faithfulness.

Perhaps the most astounding characteristic of God's personality is that He is triune. The Christian believes that God is three co-existent, co-eternal persons in one, who are equal in purpose and in essence, but differ in function.

The God of the Christian also is a God of power, evidenced by His works in creation and providence. Hebrews 1:10 declares, "In the beginning, Lord, You established the earth, and the heavens are the works of your hands." Christian theology asserts that God is the source of all things and that He created the cosmos out of His own mind, according to His plan.

God also demonstrates His power by moving His world to a purposeful end. Each created thing has an appointed destiny—God has a plan for His world, and nothing takes Him by surprise. The Bible is emphatic on this point. Romans 9:25-26 says, "I will call 'Not-My-People,' 'My-People,' and she who is 'Unloved,' 'Beloved.' And it will be in the place where they were told, you are not my people, there they will be called sons of the living God." Scripture makes it clear that God manifests His power by a sovereign and holy plan—a plan which generally collides with the plans of men.

GOD AS JUDGE

The judgment of God is not a popular subject—even among Christians. A great majority of people abhor the thought that the "God of love" could also be the "God of wrath." However, one cannot read the Bible without encountering the judgment of God.

The holiness of God necessitates the judgment of God. Christian theists agree that God must be a judge because His holy nature is antithetical to sin. Such acts in the Bible as the great flood (Genesis 6:17-7:24), the destruction of Sodom and Gomorrah (Genesis 19), the smiting of Nadab and Abihu (Leviticus 10:1-7), the fall of the Canaanites (Leviticus 18-20), and the fall of Israel (2 Kings

God's holiness requires that He judge the world for its sins.

17) and Judah (2 Chronicles 36) are all demonstrations of God's judgment as motivated by His holy nature.

> The holiness of God necessitates the judgment of God.

Christianity teaches that God is fair and always right because His nature is perfect. God is not a giant bully or a cosmic killjoy brooding in the heavens, waiting for an opportunity to spoil everyone's fun. The Bible teaches that God is truly interested in good winning over evil, and in holiness being the victor over moral depravity. In short, God judges people because they are sinners. The Bible is clear in communicating that God does not take pleasure in the judgment of the wicked (Ezekiel 33:11), but the wicked must be judged because God is holy (Jude 15).

GOD AS REDEEMER

Only one thing can protect people from God's wrath on the day of judgment: God's mercy. In His mercy, God has provided an advocate for every individual—an advocate so righteous that He washes away the sin that should condemn every person. God as the Redeemer, in the person of Christ, saves people from His wrath.

The central theme of redemption is the love of God. John 3:16 tells us, "For God loved the world in this way: He gave His only Son, so that everyone who believes in Him will not perish but have eternal life." Using John 3:16 as a text

> Only one thing can protect people from God's wrath on the day of judgment: God's mercy.

for portraying God's love, theologian Floyd Barackman points out the following characteristics of this love:

1. **God's love is universal.** God loves every nation, tribe, race, class, and gender equally. There were no social prejudices when God offered His Son. Christ died for the rich and for the poor, for the free and for the enslaved, for the old and for the young, for the beautiful and for the ugly.
2. **God's love is gracious.** God loves sinners even when they hate Him and do not deserve His love. Romans 5:8 clearly outlines the nature of God's love: "But God proves His own love for us in that while we were still

sinners Christ died for us!" How could God love the sinner? This question is answered by the Christian doctrine of grace. Christianity declares that God's love and mercy are so awesome that He can love the sinner while hating the sin.

Christ's death was a sacrifice based on the Old Testament concept of atonement for sins.

3. **God's love is sacrificial.** God did not send His only Son to earth just to be a good example or simply to be a teacher, but to be a perfect and atoning sacrifice for sin. Christ's substitutionary death was sacrificial and closely resembles the Old Testament concept of atonement. The main difference between Old Testament atonement and the New Testament concept is that in the Old Testament it was temporary, whereas in the New Testament Christ atoned for sins once and for all. Through the death of Christ, God has reconciled the world to Himself and offered a way for His wrath to be appeased (Colossians 1:20)—man now must be reconciled to God through faith in Christ (2 Corinthians 5:20).

4. **God's love is beneficial.** For all those who receive Christ (John 1:12), for all those who are born from above (John 3:3), for all those who believe (John 3:16), there await certain eternal benefits given by God. Scripture declares that through God's grace, the believer will not be condemned (Romans 3:24) and will not be captive to sin (Romans 6:11). Further, the believer is a new creation (2 Corinthians 5:17) who has been declared righteous (2 Corinthians 5:21), redeemed (1 Peter 1:18), forgiven (Ephesians 1:7) and who is the recipient of the gift of eternal life (John 3:16).

CONCLUSION

Christian theology is Christ-centered. The God who loved the world so that "He gave His only Son" has allowed for a personal relationship between Himself and fallen man. Theoretical atheistic possibilities belittle the God who has revealed Himself propositionally through His creation and His word and who has sacrificed His incarnate and holy Son. If the story is true, then the world that lives in unbelief should be fearful, for it sits under the judgment of God until it recognizes and experiences the ever-faithful promise of Jesus: "Listen! I stand at the door and knock. If anyone hears My voice and opens the door, I will come in to him and have dinner with him, and he with Me" (Revelation 3:20).

RECOMMENDED READING FOR ADVANCED STUDY:
THEOLOGY

Beisner, E. Calvin. *Answers for Atheists, Agnostics, and Other Thoughtful Skeptics: Dialogs About Christian Faith and Life.* Wheaton, Ill.: Crossway Books, 1993.

Bruce, F. F. *Jesus and Christian Origins Outside the New Testament.* Grand Rapids, Mich.: Eerdmans, 1974.

Carson, D. A. *The Gagging of God.* Grand Rapids, Mich.: Zondervan, 1996.

Geisler, Norman L. and William E. Nix. *A General Introduction to the Bible.* Chicago: Moody Press, 1977.

Glynn, Patrick. *God—The Evidence: The Reconciliation of Faith and Reason in a Postsecular World.* Rocklin, Ca.: Prima Publishing, 1999.

Harrison, Everett, Geoffrey W. Bromiley, and Carl F. H. Henry, eds. *Baker's Dictionary of Theology.* Grand Rapids, Mich.: Baker, 1975.

ENDNOTES

1. Stephen D. Schwarz, "Introduction—Philosophy," *The Intellectuals Speak Out About God,* ed. Roy Abraham Varghese (Dallas, TX: Lewis and Stanley, 1984), p. 98.

2. James Orr, *The Christian View of God and the World* (Edinburgh: Andrew Elliot, 1897), p. 111.

3. Millard J. Erickson, *Christian Theology,* three volumes (Grand Rapids, Mich.: Baker Book House, 1983), vol 1, p. 153.

4. Carl F.H. Henry, *God, Revelation and Authority,* six volumes (Waco, Tex.: Word Books, 1976ff), vol. 2, p.11.

5. Ibid., p. 15.

6. Charles Darwin, *Autobiography* (New York: Dover Publishing, 1958), p. 59.

7. C.S. Lewis, *Broadcast Talks* (London: 1946), p. 37-8.

CHAPTER 3

Philosophy

KEY QUESTION

What is real, and what is true?

KEY IDEA

The single most important philosophical
truth in the Bible is that Jesus Christ is the
Logos of God.

KEY QUOTE

"The crucial problem is that some thinkers place
their trust in a set of assumptions in their search for
truth, while other thinkers place their trust in a
quite different set of assumptions."
—WARREN C. YOUNG

SUMMARY

The philosophical quest that most appeals to Christians is the attempt to obey 2 Corinthians 10:4-5, "We demolish arguments and every high-minded thing that is raised up against the knowledge of God, taking every thought captive to the obedience of Christ." Philosophy is not inherently non-Christian. What makes some philosophy non-Christian is what the Bible refers to as "philosophy and empty deceit." That is, philosophy "based on human tradition, based on the elemental forces of the world, and not based on Christ" (Colossians 2:8). The single most important philosophical truth in the Bible is that Jesus Christ is the Logos (word, or mind) of God. Christian philosophy says Christ the Logos is the explanation for the universe and everything in it. The major charge against Christianity in general and Christian philosophy in particular, is that it is unscientific. Christians claim that the Christian doctrines of God, creation, Logos, design, purpose, law, order, and life are consistent with the findings of science, history, and personal experience in a way that the vain and deceitful philosophies of dialectical materialism and philosophical naturalism will never be.

Some people assume that the Christian worldview cannot possibly have a philosophy of its own, since it requires faith in biblical revelation. How can Christians, who must postulate existence or reality outside the material realm, ever hope to prove their beliefs true, reasonable, rational, and worth living and dying for?

Unfortunately, some Christians adopt just such an attitude—conceding that their faith is indefensible. They attempt to avoid the whole problem by stating that what they believe is "beyond reason." These Christians point to Colossians 2:8, where Paul writes, "Be careful that no one takes you captive through philosophy and empty deceit . . . ," and from this they draw the conclusion that God does not want us to meddle in such a vain and "deceitful" discipline as philosophy. However, people who point to this verse as a warning against philosophy often omit the rest of the verse, in which Paul describes the kind of philosophy he is warning against, namely, philosophy "based on human tradition, based on the elemental forces of the world, and not based on Christ."

> **The Bible does not ask the Christian to abandon reason in accepting its truth.**

The Bible does not ask the Christian to abandon reason in accepting its truth. "'Come,'" records Isaiah, "'let us discuss this,' says the Lord. 'Though your sins are like scarlet, they will be as white as snow'" (Isaiah 1:18). 1 Peter 3:15 encourages Christians to understand and be able to present logical, compelling reasons for their hope in Christ. But is this possible? Is Christian faith and, more specifically, Christian philosophy defensible?

C.E.M. Joad, who lived most of his life believing that the concept of God was unacceptable, finally concluded, "It is because . . . the religious view of the universe seems to me to cover more of the facts of experience than any other that I have been gradually led to embrace it."[1] He concluded his long personal pilgrimage by admitting, "I now believe that the balance of reasonable considerations tells heavily in favor of the religious, even of the Christian view of the world."[2] This is the same Joad who appeared on BBC radio with humanist Bertrand Russell attacking Christianity.

Many who reflect honestly on the deeper things of life—"Where did I come from? Why am I here? Where am I going?"—discover that Christianity answers more questions more completely than any other worldview. Those who earnestly seek truth will ultimately find themselves face-to-face with the God of the Bible. It is all well and good to debate whether God exists, but for the average person the debate is a moot point. They don't require reasoned argument because most people are aware of His existence in their very souls. Even today the vast majority of human beings in the world believe in a God (some polls place the figure as high as 95 percent). Paul found this to be true in Athens as well (Acts 17:23). People tend to believe the most likely solution to a problem. That's why most people believe, "In the beginning God created the heavens and the earth" (Genesis 1:1) and "everything in it" (Acts 17:24). Jean Piaget, a child psychologist, has found that a seven year-old almost instinctively believes that everything in the universe has a purpose. It makes more (common) sense to believe Genesis 1:1 than to believe that a series of cosmic accidents brought about the orderly, beautiful, meaningful cosmos.

> *"Thou hast formed us for Thyself, and our hearts are restless till they find rest in Thee."*
>
> —St. Augustine

FAITH AND EPISTEMOLOGY

The basic tenets of Christian philosophy can be demonstrated to be rational, for they are held by average, rational men and women. But surely, Christianity must still run into an epistemological problem—how does the Christian know without clashing with science and experience? This is the question of epistemology, or how we know what we say we know. In addition, the Christian must often answer the related question: How can the knowledge we gain through faith in biblical revelation compare to knowledge gained by a scientific investigation of the universe?

The answer is not as difficult as you might imagine. When all is said and done, all knowing requires faith. Faith precedes reason or, as W. J. Neidhardt puts it, "Faith correctly viewed is that illumination by which true rationality begins."[3] While some Secular Humanists like to portray science as the primary source for knowledge and faith in biblical revelation as some blind second-class epistemology or even superstition, the fact remains that all methods of knowing ultimately rely on certain assumptions. Edward T. Ramsdell writes, "The natural man is no less certainly a man of faith than the spiritual, but his faith is in the ultimacy of something other than the Word of God. The spiritual man is no less certainly a man of reason than the natural, but his reason, like that of every man, functions within the perspective of his faith."[4]

The basic problem of philosophy is not the problem of faith versus reason. "The crucial problem," says Warren C. Young, "is that some thinkers place their trust in a set of assumptions in their search for truth, while other thinkers place their trust in a quite different set of assumptions."[5] That is, Secular

Knowledge gained through the scientific investigation of the universe rests on a specific set of assumptions.

Humanists (atheists) place their trust in certain findings of science and experience, neither of which can be rationally demonstrated to be the source of all truth. Christians also put some faith in science, history, and personal experience, but they know such avenues for discovering truth are not infallible. Christians know that men of science make mistakes and scientific journals can practice discrimination against views considered dangerous. Christians know that history can be perverted, distorted or twisted, and that some personal experiences are not a good source of fact or knowledge. On the other hand, Christians believe that biblical revelation is true and that God would not fool or mislead His children.

It should be stressed that Christian philosophy does not throw out reason or tests for truth. Christianity says the New Testament is true because

> Christianity says the New Testament is true because its truths can be tested.

its truths can be tested. Christians aren't asking the non-believer to believe a revelation of old wives' fables, but instead to consider historical evidences that reason itself can employ, much as an attorney builds a case using evidences to determine questions of fact. Christian epistemology is based on special revelation which, in turn, is based on history, the law of evidence, and the science of archaeology.

Up to this point we have established two things regarding Christian philosophy:

• Many hold it to be the most rational of all worldviews.

• It requires no more faith than any other philosophy.

Indeed, one could argue that it takes a great deal more faith to believe in the spontaneous generation doctrine of Secular Humanism and Marxism or the randomness of all nature (i.e., that the universe happened by accident) than it does to accept the Christian doctrine of Creator/Creation.

RECONCILING SCIENCE AND CHRISTIAN PHILOSOPHY

At the outset of this chapter, it may have appeared that reconciling supernaturalism with science would be difficult. However, in light of the previous discussion, little reconciliation, if any, is necessary.

The wise Christian philosopher recognizes the scientific method as a limited, but valuable, ally. In addition to lending support for the teleological argument (discerning God from the design evident in Creation), science also shores up the cosmological argument (about the origin and nature of the universe) and raises serious questions about whether or not atoms are material particles (which doesn't bode well for either naturalism or materialism).

"Christianity was 'the mother of modern science.'"

—FRANCIS SCHAEFFER

Joad reinforces the idea that science does not threaten Christianity, stating, "It has often been represented that the conclusions of science are hostile to the tenets of religion. Whatever grounds there may have been for such a view in the past, it is hard to see with what good reason such a contention could be sustained today."[6] Stephen D. Schwarz cites four specific scientific discoveries that support the conclusion that God exists: the Second Law of Thermodynamics, the impossibility of spontaneous generation of life from non-life, genetic information theory (DNA), and the Anthropic Principle (that the cosmos is "fine-tuned" to accommodate human life).

"In science we have been reading only the notes to a poem; in Christianity we find the poem itself."

—C.S. LEWIS

For the Christian, then, science need not be an enemy. Indeed, science should be accepted as a fairly successful means to obtain knowledge about God's design in the universe. As C.S. Lewis says, "In science we have been reading only the notes to a poem; in Christianity we find the poem itself." [7]

THE ORIGIN OF SCIENCE

An examination of the history of modern science reaffirms the supernaturalist's premise that science is not hostile to his position. Modern science was founded by men who viewed the world from a Christian perspective. Neither the Marxist nor the humanist worldview, with their corresponding beliefs that the universe was

brought about by a series of accidents, could serve as a fitting base for modern science. Francis Schaeffer writes, "Since the world had been created by a reasonable God, [scientists] were not surprised to find a correlation between themselves as observers and the thing observed—that is, between subject and object. . . . Without this foundation, modern Western science would not have been born." [8]

Christianity was "the mother of modern science." [9] Norman L. Geisler and J. Kerby Anderson's *Origin Science* includes a chapter

Our confidence in the unchanging Law of Gravity makes space flight possible.

entitled "The Supernatural Roots of Modern Science." Both English philosopher Alfred North Whitehead and American physicist J. Robert Oppenheimer defended this view. Philosopher and historian of science Stanley L. Jaki notes that historically the belief in creation and the Creator was the moment of truth for science: "This belief formed the bedrock on which science rose." [10] Jaki has powerfully defended this position in *The Origin of Science* and *The Savior of Science*.

Re-examine the statements by Schaeffer and Jaki for a moment. Notice that each claim is grounded on the fact that science assumed an orderly universe. If man believed the universe to be disorderly or chaotic, he never would have bothered with science, which relies on matter to behave in certain meaningful ways under controlled conditions. On earth, we always expect an apple to fall down rather than up, because we believe in a consistent law—the Law of Gravity. Lewis says men became scientific because they expected Law in Nature, and "they expected Law in Nature because they believed in a Legislator."[11] In other words, the origin of modern science itself provides grounds for the teleological argument—the argument from design to Designer.

METAPHYSICS: ONTOLOGY/COSMOLOGY

The Christian view of metaphysics—of ultimate reality (ontology and cosmology)—is part of what C. S. Lewis termed "mere Christianity." There are certain things virtually all Christians believe, and one is that God is the supreme source of all being and reality. He is the ultimate reality and because He is, we are. The space-time creation, says Carl F.H. Henry, depends on the Creator-God "for its actuality, its meaning and its purpose."[12] This creation is intelligible because God is intelligent, and we can understand the creation and Creator because He made us in His image with the capacity to understand Him and His intelligent order.

For the Christian, matter exists but it is not the ultimate substance. It is real, but it is not ultimate reality. It is not eternal. Rather, the material universe was created on purpose out of the mind of the living Logos (John 1:1-4), and all the cosmos, existing independently of God, relies on God for its very existence and explanation. In other words, the Christian explanation for the world of matter or nature is that the supernatural created the natural. And since the supernatural God of the Bible is a rational, purposeful, powerful God, the created universe itself contains such qualities. It is no accident that at every level of the cosmos—sub-atomic, atomic, organic, inorganic, sub-human, human, earth, moon, sun, stars, galaxies—all things manifest

> The Christian explanation for the world of matter or nature is that the supernatural created the natural.

amazing order and rationality that can be reasonably explained only as the result of a deliberate, creative act of God.

Christianity considers entirely irrational the notion that the orderly cosmos is the result of a series of accidents, chance, or random happenings. Such a position is tantamount to having a bridge, an airplane, an automobile, or a skyscraper, without an architect, plan, or engineer. It doesn't happen that way in the real world, only in the minds of those who lack faith in the supernatural and in the Bible.

The early verses of John 1 contain the Christian's metaphysics in a nutshell. "In the beginning [of the cosmos] was the Word [Logos, mind, reason, thought, wisdom, intelligence, idea, law, order, purpose, design], and the Word was with God, and the Word was God. He was with God in the beginning. All things were created through Him; and apart from Him not one thing was created that has been created. In Him was life, and that life was the light of men" (John 1:1-4).

To believe that the universe has no designer is as irrational as thinking that a bridge comes about by chance.

The flow of this passage sets forth the parameters of Christian philosophy: mind before matter, God before man, plan and design before creation, life from life, and enlightenment from the Light. The orderly universe was conceived in the orderly and rational mind of God before it was created. Without the Logos there would be no cosmos. From the Christian perspective it is no surprise to see philosophers and scientists refer to the universe as a manifestation of mathematical law, order, design, beauty, etc. This is the way it was created "in the beginning."

Young says, "Christian realists are contingent dualists but not eternal dualists. They hold that there are two kinds of substance: Spirit (or God) and matter which was created by God *ex nihilo* as Augustine suggested. Matter is not spirit, nor is it reducible to spirit, but its existence is always dependent upon God Who created it out of nothing."[13] Young chooses to use the term "Christian realism" to represent the Christian philosophy. In an effort to stress the existence of something other than the material, we employ the term "supernaturalism." Regardless of the name, true Christian philosophy requires a metaphysics consistent with biblical teaching.

MIND-BODY PROBLEM AND THE MENTAL PROOF

The supernaturalist believes that the mind, or consciousness, exists as a separate entity from the purely physical. The Christian believes that his mind is a reflection of the Universal Mind that created the universe *ex nihilo,* and he sees the mind as an additional proof for the existence of the supernatural. Most men perceive their thinking process as something different from the material world. Young says, "Man is so made that his spirit may operate upon and influence his body, and his body is so made that it may operate upon his mind or spirit."[14]

> **Supernaturalism** is the belief that the mind, or consciousness, exists as a separate entity from the purely physical.

This distinction between brain and mind implies a distinction about the whole order of things: matter exists, and something other than matter exists. As James Buswell comments, "We find in the created universe an important difference between beings which think, and beings which are spatially extended, or spiritual beings and material beings. . . . In the body and mind of man we see integrated interaction between the spiritual thinking being, and the material extended being."[15]

> *"Man is so made that his spirit may operate upon and influence his body, and his body is so made that it may operate upon his mind or spirit."*
> —WARREN C. YOUNG

Many Christian thinkers believe this distinction between the brain and the mind is intuitively obvious, and this is the beginning of the mental proof for the existence of a Higher Mind that created our minds. Other Christian thinkers begin with the untenability of the materialist position that the mind is only a material phenomenon and draw the conclusion that since the materialist explanation is irrational, the supernatural explanation must be the acceptable position. Again, science aids the Christian philosopher in undermining the materialist worldview. Writes Buswell, "The mind is not the brain. The 'brain track' psychology has failed. . . . It is a known fact that if certain parts of the brain are destroyed, and the functions corresponding to those parts impaired, the functions may be taken up by other parts of the brain. There is no exact correspondence between mind and brain."[16]

Sir John Eccles has made a voluminous contribution to this discussion in recent years. His three works, *The Self and Its Brain* (with Karl Popper), *The Human Mystery* and *The Human Psyche* are considered classics in the field. Eccles maintains that having a mind means one is conscious, and that consciousness is a mental event, not a material event. He further contends that there are two distinct orders—the brain is in the material world and the mind is in the "world of subjective experience."

> The materialist explanation is irrational.

Lewis cuts to the heart of the materialist and naturalist dilemma when he writes, "The Naturalists have been engaged in thinking about Nature. They have not attended to the fact that they were thinking. The moment one attends to this it is obvious that one's own thinking cannot be merely a natural event, and that therefore something other than Nature exists. The Supernatural is not remote and abstruse: it is a matter of daily and hourly experience, as intimate as breathing."[17]

D. Elton Trueblood believes that supernaturalism is unavoidable: "How can nature include mind as an integral part unless it is grounded in mind? If mind were seen as something alien or accidental, the case would be different, but the further we go in modern science the clearer it becomes that mental experience is no strange offshoot. Rather it is something which is deeply rooted in the entire structure."[18] Implied, then, is the existence of a God that could create an

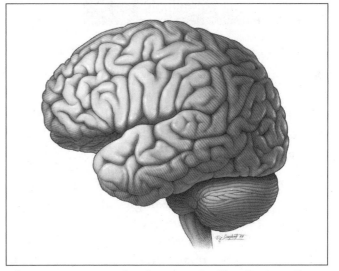

"There is no exact correspondence between mind and brain."—James Oliver Buswell, Jr.

entire structure with mind as an integral part. Once an individual grants the existence of an orderly mind separate from the physical universe, belief in the Ultimate Mind becomes the only rational option.

Christians must remember, however, that God is much more than an "Ultimate Mind." The mental proof may help to establish the existence of God, but the God of rational "proofs" alone is unworthy of worship—only the Christian God, in all His power and holiness, elicits awe and love in their proper proportion.

CONCLUSION

Supernaturalism is more than a philosophy in the narrow sense. Christian philosophy represents a worldview that is consistent with the Bible throughout. In the end, everyone must choose between a materialist/naturalist worldview and a supernaturalist worldview—and the choice will create repercussions for every aspect of the individual's life. Christian philosophy embraces the meaningful, purposeful life, a life in which each of us shapes his or her beliefs according to a coherent, reasonable, truthful worldview. A person who holds such a worldview will not be tossed to and fro by every secularist doctrine. Dr. Young says:

> Christian philosophy represents a worldview that is consistent with the Bible throughout.

> In the same way it can be said that the Christian philosopher and theologian must be acquainted with the contending worldviews of his age. Philosophy, after all, is a way of life, and the Christian believes that he has the true way—the true pattern for living. It is the task of the Christian leader to understand the ideologies of his day so that he may be able to meet their challenge. The task is a never-ending one, for, although the Christian's worldview does not change, the world about him does. Thus the task of showing the relevance of the Christian realistic philosophy to a world in process is one which requires eternal vigilance. To such a task, to such an ideal, the Christian leader must dedicate himself.[19]

RECOMMENDED READING FOR ADVANCED STUDY: PHILOSOPHY

Geisler, Norman L. and Winfried Corduan. *Philosophy of Religion.* 2nd ed. Grand Rapids, Mich.: Baker Hook House, 1988.

Johnson, Phillip E. *Reason in the Balance: The Case Against Naturalism in Science, Education and Law.* Downers Grove, Ill.: InterVarsity Press, 1995.

Nash, Ronald H. *Life's Ultimate Questions: An Introduction to Philosophy.* Grand Rapids, Mich.: Zondervan, 1999.

Moreland, J. P. *Scaling the Secular City.* Grand Rapids, Mich.: Baker Book House, 1987.

Plantinga, Alvin. *Warranted Christian Belief.* New York: Oxford University Press, 2000.

ENDNOTES

1. C.E.M. Joad, *The Recovery of Belief* (London: Faber and Faber Limited, 1955), p. 16.

2. Ibid., p. 22.

3. Carl F.H. Henry, *God, Revelation and Authority,* six volumes (Waco, Tex.: Word Books, 1976), vol. 1, p. 169. Henry mentions W.J. Neidhardt's work, "Faith, the Unrecognized Partner of Science and Religion," as the source for his comments.

4. Edward T. Ramsdell, *The Christian Perspective* (New York: Abingdon-Cokesbury Press, 1950), p. 42.

5. Warren C. Young, *A Christian Approach to Philosophy* (Grand Rapids, Mich.: Baker, [1954] 1975), p. 37.

6. Joad, *The Recovery of Belief,* p. 107.

7. *A Mind Awake: An Anthology of C.S. Lewis,* ed. Clyde S. Kilby (New York and London: Harcourt, Brace & World, 1968), p. 240.

8. Francis A. Schaeffer, *How Should We Then Live?* (Old Tappan, N.J.: Fleming H. Revell, 1976), p. 134.

9. Ibid., p. 134.

10. Stanley L. Jaki, *The Road of Science* (South Bend, Ind.: Regnery Gateway, 1979) P. 143.

11. *A Mind Awake,* ed. Kilby, p. 234.

12. Henry, *God, Revelation and Authority,* vol. 5, p. 336.

13. Young, *A Christian Approach to Philosophy,* p. 37.

14. Ibid., p. 120.

15. James Oliver Buswell, Jr,. *A Christian View of Being and Knowing* (Grand Rapids, Mich.: Zondervan, 1960), p. 8.

16. Ibid., p. 142.

17. *A Mind Awake,* ed. Kilby, p. 205.

18. D. Elton Trueblood, *Philosophy of Religion* (Grand Rapids, Mich.: Baker Book House, 1957), p. 206.

19. Young, *A Christian Approach to Philosophy,* pp. 228-9.

CHAPTER 4

Biology

KEY QUESTION

What is the origin of life?

KEY IDEA

Science is re-learning an old lesson:
the more one discovers about the universe,
the more one discovers design.

KEY QUOTE

"When all relevant lines of evidence are taken into account, and
all the problems squarely faced, I think we must conclude that
life owes its inception to a source
outside of nature."

—Dean Kenyon

SUMMARY

When it comes to the origin of living systems and the great diversity of life, biblical Christianity maintains that to adequately account for the design observed on every level in nature, it postulates a Designer, a Lawgiver, and an orderly First Cause. Christians believe the creationist model as described in Scripture better fits the facts of science than the evolutionary model. Christianity trusts the authority of Genesis as well as declarations about creation, such as those in Mark 10:6 and Colossians 1:16. Science and Christianity are demonstrated to be compatible and to declare in unison that God "created all things" (Ephesians 3:9). The Bible gives us information about God and His universe, while science gives us information only about God's universe.

Perhaps no other aspect of Christianity has troubled believers more in the last century than the question of origins. Because many biologists treat evolution as a scientific fact, Christians have struggled to reconcile their faith in the Bible with the "fact" that man and all living things evolved from a single speck of life. This reconciliation is impossible from a rational perspective. Christians who believe that God created the first glimmer of life on earth and then directed its evolution to generate man (the belief known as theistic evolution) must take substantial liberties in interpreting the Bible, and they face most of the same arguments Christians use against atheistic evolution.

Jesus Christ declares in Mark 10:6, "But at the beginning of creation God 'made them male and female.'" Theistic evolutionists have, through semantic acrobatics, managed to interpret this verse and others like it so that they appear to support the evolutionary position. Theistic evolutionists contend that the term creation simply means that God created the first spark of life and then directed His creation through the vehicle of evolution.

Thus, some Christians believe that the Bible does not necessarily deny evolutionary theory as an explanation for origins. This may appear to be a tenable position when discussing only

The idea that all living things evolved from a single speck of life cannot be reconciled logically with the message of the Bible.

verses concerned strictly with the question of origins. However, when one examines the entire message of the Bible, the doctrine of theistic evolution severely undermines the Christian understanding of God and man's place in His universe.

For example, while it is true that God is capable of anything that is logically possible, so that He could have used evolution to generate all species, why would

Because the Bible teaches that Jesus is the sinless counterpart to Adam, it is difficult to view the story of the garden of Eden merely as an allegory.

He employ such an inefficient (and often totally ineffective) mechanism? If God designed the world to operate according to specific natural laws requiring minimal routine interference, why would He use an evolutionary mechanism that would require His constant meddling with the development of life? Further, such a mechanism seems an especially cruel method for creating man. As Jacques Monod notes, natural selection is the "blindest and most cruel way of evolving new species."[1]

More important, if evolution is true, then the story of the garden of Eden and original sin must be viewed as nothing more than allegory, a view that undermines the significance of Christ's sinless life and sacrificial death on the cross. Why? Because the Bible presents Jesus as analogous to Adam. The condemnation and corruption brought on us by Adam's sin are the counterparts of the justification and sanctification made possible for us by Christ's righteousness and death (Romans 5:12-19). If Adam was not a historical individual, and if his fall into sin was not historical, then the biblical doctrines of sin and of Christ's atonement for it collapse.

> Christians who wish to integrate faith and reason would do well to abandon evolution as a rational explanation for the origin of species.

Of course, this conclusion is unacceptable for the Christian. Thus, it is our contention that the proper Christian worldview requires a belief in the Creator as He is literally portrayed in Genesis. For a Christian to have believed in creation forty, thirty, or even twenty years ago might have seemed radical because, until recently, evolution appeared to be unassailable scientifically. Understandably, many Christians turned to theistic evolution as the only means of reconciling their reason with their faith. Today, however, the scientific objections to evolution are so strong that Christians who wish to integrate faith and reason would do well to abandon evolution as a rational explanation for the origin of species. The reasons for this will be explained later in this chapter.

CHRISTIANITY AND SCIENCE

The roots of modern science are grounded in a Christian view of the world. This is not surprising, since science is based on the assumption that the universe is orderly and can be expected to act according to specific, discoverable laws. An ordered, lawful universe would seem to be the effect of an intelligent Cause, which was precisely the belief of many early scientists.

> The roots of modern science are grounded in a Christian view of the world.

Renowned philosopher and historian of science Stanley L. Jaki specifies that "from Copernicus to Newton it was not deism but Christian theism that served as a principal factor helping the scientific enterprise reach self-sustaining maturity."[2] Inherent in this early scientific dependence on the orderliness of the world was the belief that the world was ordered by a Divine Creator. As Langdon Gilkey points out, "The religious idea of a transcendent creator actually made possible rather than hindered the progress of the scientific understanding of the natural order."[3] Modern evolutionists have lost sight of this order. According to their perspective, all life is the result of chance processes.

This problem of perspective causes many evolutionists to lose sight of the marvels that abound in our universe. Whereas earlier scientists accepted Christianity and therefore were able to recognize the order of their world as a reflection of the Creator's omniscience, evolutionists must now view everything as fortunate accidents (with emphasis on chance instead of cosmos). Creationists understand that the vast order and design in our world point unequivocally toward a Designer and Creator. Thus, creationists use teleology—design in nature—to support creationism.

> "The religious idea of a transcendent creator actually made possible rather than hindered the progress of the scientific understanding of the natural order."
> —LANGDON GILKEY

TELEOLOGY SUPPORTS CREATIONISM

William Paley presented the most famous version of the teleological argument—that of the watch and the watchmaker. Since the nineteenth century, however, it has been widely believed that Paley's argument for a universal Designer was effectively answered by the philosopher David Hume. Hume claimed that Paley's analogy between living things and machines was unfounded and unrealistic and, therefore, that life does not need an intelligent designer, as machines do. Hume's reply to Paley caused many people to discredit the teleological argument in all its forms, which also contributed to the willingness of science to ignore design in nature and suggest that all life arose by chance.

William Paley argued that a watch, like Creation, evidences design and purpose and that no one could rationally argue that either always had existed or had happened by chance.

But science can no longer ignore teleology. Indeed, science has recently discovered that life really is analogous to the most complex of machines, thereby reinforcing Paley's argument. Michael Denton, a molecular biologist, states, "Paley was not only right in asserting the existence of an analogy between life and machines, but was also remarkably prophetic in guessing that the technological ingenuity realized in living systems is vastly in excess of anything yet accomplished by man."[4]

"Over the past four decades modern biochemistry has uncovered the secrets of the cell. . . . The result of these cumulative efforts to investigate the cell—to investigate life at the molecular level—is a loud, clear, piercing cry of 'design!'"[5]

—MICHAEL J. BEHE, PH.D.

Science is re-learning an old lesson: the more one discovers about the universe, the more one discovers design. Many notable scientists inadvertently support Paley nowadays as they describe the design in nature revealed to them through science. Physicist Paul Davies, who does not profess to be a Christian, supports teleology—and ultimately creationism—when he says, "Every advance in fundamental physics seems to uncover yet another facet of order."[6]

> "Every advance in fundamental physics seems to uncover yet another facet of order."
> —PAUL DAVIES

At first, this seems to be an obvious conclusion of little significance. But strict evolution demands chance rather than a Law-maker as the guiding force. When a world-class non-Christian scientist like Davies declares that the universe cannot be viewed as a product of chance, it is a severe blow to materialistic evolutionary theory.

When one truly understands the ordered complexity of life, it is hard to imagine chance producing even bacterial cells, which are the simplest living systems. Denton explains: "Although the tiniest bacterial cells are incredibly small, weighing less than 10(-12) grams, each is in effect a veritable micro-miniaturized factory containing thousands of exquisitely designed pieces of intricate molecular machinery, made up altogether of one hundred thousand million atoms, far more complicated than any machine built by man and absolutely without parallel in the non-living world."[7] As Paley

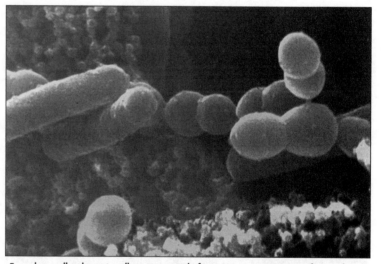

Even the smallest bacteria cells are composed of an intricate arrangement of more than 100,000,000,000,000 atoms, undermining the notion that any living thing is truly simple.

pointed out almost two centuries ago, this type of design requires an intelligent mind—chance processes cannot produce such intricate order.

DNA: CREATED OR EVOLVED?

The existence and properties of deoxyribonucleic acid (DNA) support creationism both through the teleological argument and by demonstrating evolutionary theory's inability to explain crucial aspects of life. DNA contains the genetic information code and is a crucial part of all living matter, yet evolutionary theory is powerless to explain how it came into existence, let alone why DNA evinces such phenomenal design.

This teleological quality of DNA is overwhelming. Charles Thaxton believes DNA is the most powerful indicator of intelligent design: "Is there any basis in experience for an intelligent cause for the origin of life? Yes! It is the analogy between the base sequences in DNA and alphabetical letter sequences in a book. . . . there is a structural identity between the DNA code and a written language."[8] That is, we can assume DNA is the product of intelligence because it is analogous to human languages, which are—without exception—the product of intelligent minds.

DNA = deoxyribonucleic acid

Even excluding the teleological nature of DNA, its very existence severely undermines evolutionary theory. Walter Brown points out, "DNA can only be produced with the help of at least 20 different types of proteins. But these proteins can only be produced at the direction of DNA. Since each requires the other, a satisfactory explanation for the origin of one must also explain the origin of the other. Apparently, this entire manufacturing system came into existence simultaneously. This implies Creation."[9]

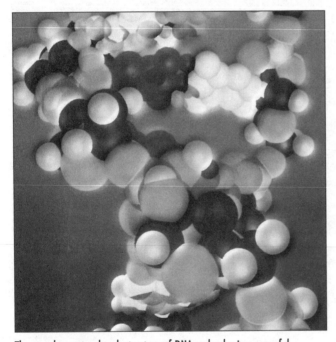

The complex, yet ordered, structure of DNA molecules is a powerful indicator of intelligent design.

DNA obviously presents one of the most pressing problems for evolutionists. It is an intensely complex substance, yet it must be present in the very earliest forms of living matter. How can evolutionists explain this? They cannot. In fact, no one has shown how life itself could arise from non-living chemicals, let alone such a complex aspect of life as DNA. This inability to demonstrate spontaneous generation (the development of life from non-life) is another key weakness in evolutionary theory.

SPONTANEOUS GENERATION

For the atheistic evolutionist's belief to be rational, the major problem biology must overcome is the impossibility of spontaneous generation. In order for life to have arisen due to random processes, at some point in time non-living matter must have come alive.

> The major problem biology must overcome is the impossibility of spontaneous generation.

Many evolutionists point to the work of Alexander Oparin in defense of spontaneous genera-tion. Oparin described a theory that supposedly allowed for chance processes working in a prebiotic soup to give rise to life. Unfortunately for evolutionists, this theory is rapidly being refuted by science.

In fact, the further science progresses, the more unlikely spontaneous generation seems. Dean Kenyon, a biochemist and a former chemical evolutionist, now writes, "When all relevant lines of evidence are taken into account, and all the problems squarely faced, I think we must conclude that life owes its inception to a source outside of nature."[10] He bases this conclusion on four premises:

(1) **the impossibility of the spontaneous origin of genetic information,**
(2) **the fact that most attempts to duplicate the conditions necessary for chemical evolution yield non-biological material,**
(3) **the unfounded nature of the belief that prebiotic conditions encouraged a trend toward the formation of L amino acids, and**
(4) **the geochemical evidence that O_2 existed in significant amounts in the earth's early atmosphere (organic com-pounds decompose when O_2 is present).**

Brown also believes the existence of O_2 creates an insurmountable problem for chemical evolutionists: "If the earth, early in its alleged evolution, had oxygen in its atmosphere, the chemicals needed for life to begin would have been removed by oxidation. But if there had been no oxygen, then there would have been no ozone in the upper atmosphere. Without this ozone, life would be quickly destroyed by the sun's ultraviolet radiation."[11] Ozone and life, therefore, must have originated simultaneously—at the time of creation.

THE SECOND LAW OF THERMODYNAMICS

Another major hurdle for evolutionary theory involves the Second Law of Thermodynamics. In order to understand the clash between evolution and the Second Law of Thermodynamics, we must first understand a few of the implications of the Second Law. A.E. Wilder-Smith explains, "The Second Law of Thermodynamics states that, although the total energy in the cosmos remains constant, the amount of energy available to do useful work is always getting smaller."[13]

> *"If the icons of evolution are supposed to be our best evidence for Darwin's theory, and all of them are false or misleading, what does that tell us about the theory? Is it science, or myth?"* [12]
>
> —JONATHAN WELLS, PH.D.

This law has important implications regarding the effect of time on the orderliness of the universe. While the evolutionist calls for the universe to grow more orderly as evolution progresses, the Second Law of Thermodynamics assures us that order tends to disintegrate into disorder. Wilder-Smith puts the contrast clearly: "The theory of evolution teaches, when all the frills are removed, just the opposite to this state of affairs demanded by the Second Law of Thermodynamics."[14]

The Second Law of Thermodynamics doesn't just contradict evolution. It also reinforces the creationist explanation of man's origins. First, it suggests that the universe had a beginning. "If the entire universe is an isolated system, then, according to the Second

The Second Law of Thermodynamics implies that the universe began as a highly ordered system.

Law of Thermodynamics," says Brown, "the energy in the universe that is available for useful work has always been decreasing. However, as one goes back in time, the amount of energy available for useful work would eventually exceed the total energy in the universe that, according to the First Law of Thermodynamics, remains constant. This is an impossible condition. Therefore, it implies that the universe had a beginning."[15]

Romans 8:22-3 For we know that the whole creation has been groaning together with labor pains until now. And not only that, but we ourselves who have the Spirit as the firstfruits—we also groan within ourselves, eagerly waiting for adoption, the redemption of our bodies.

Second, it suggests that the universe began as a highly ordered system. Wilder-Smith says, "The Second Law of Thermodynamics seems thus to describe the whole situation of our present material world perfectly and the Bible very clearly confirms this description. For example, Romans 8:22-23 teaches us that the whole creation is subjected to 'vanity' or to destruction. Everything tends to go downhill to chaos and destruction as things stand today."[16]

The creationist position, then, is more in sync with science than evolutionary theory. This becomes even more obvious when one considers genetics.

THE GENE POOL AND THE LIMITS TO CHANGE

Evolutionists believe that no breeding limits exist, since life-forms must ultimately break these "species barriers" to create new species. Indeed, evolutionists see beneficial mutations as breaking all barriers to change, since these mutations supposedly can produce a vast array of structures, even a human eye, given enough time.

Unfortunately for evolutionists, however, science simply has not been able to demonstrate that any mutations break these limits to change. Pierre Paul Grasse, after studying mutations in bacteria and viruses, concludes, "What is the use of their unceasing mutations if they do not change? In sum, the mutations of bacteria and viruses are merely hereditary fluctuations around a median position; a swing to the right, a swing to the left, but no final evolutionary effect."[17]

If indeed such limits exist, then evolution is a meaningless explanation. If a species can only evolve so far before it hits a barrier and is forced to remain the same species, then no macroevolution occurs. This notion of the gene pool limiting the possible variation of species has troubled a great number of evolutionists, including Alfred Russell Wallace, one of the founders of the theory of natural selection. Wallace grew to doubt his theory later in life, largely because he became aware of Gregor Mendel's genetic laws, and could not reconcile the apparent limits to change with evolution's need for boundless development. Incredibly, Edward Deevey, Jr. also recognizes these limitations, and yet remains an evolutionist: "Some remarkable things have been done by crossbreeding and selection inside the species barrier, or within a larger circle of closely related species, such as the wheats. But wheat is still wheat, and not, for instance, grapefruit; and we can no more grow wings on pigs than hens can make cylindrical eggs."[18]

> The creationist believes the evolutionary position is opposed to reason and therefore rejects it.

How can Deevey remain an evolutionist in the face of such evidence? How can one believe in virtually unlimited change when limits abound within species? Rationally, one cannot. The creationist believes the evolutionary position is opposed to reason and therefore rejects it.

It would seem that the case against evolutionists and in favor of creationism is quite formidable—indeed, retreat appears to be the only option available to the evolutionist. Incredibly, this conclusion seems justifiable even without reference to what many consider the most powerful

Despite more than 100 years of research since Darwin's time, the fossil record still fails to substantiate his theory of evolution.

refutation of evolutionary theory: the gaps in the fossil record and the absence of transitional forms. A brief examination of this evidence should leave few doubts as to the bankruptcy of evolutionary theory.

FOSSIL GAPS AND INTERMEDIATE FORMS

So far each of our arguments has focused on whether evolution is theoretically possible. Now we turn to the question of whether the empirical evidence suggests that it happened.

Over one hundred years ago, Darwin wrote, "The geological record is extremely imperfect and this fact will to a large extent explain why we do not find intermediate varieties, connecting together all the extinct and existing forms of life by the finest graduated steps. He who rejects these views on the nature of the geological record, will rightly reject my whole theory." [19] When Darwin made this claim, he was correct in asserting that the geological record, as scientists knew it then, was imperfect. Now, almost a century and a half later, it is safe to say that the geological record has been thoroughly scrutinized. And rather than confirming Darwin's theories, the fossils condemn them.

"The evolutionary tree has no trunk." —Walter T. Brown

One reason the fossil record condemns evolutionary theory is that many complex life forms appear in the very earliest rocks without any indication of forms from which they could have evolved. Creatures without ancestors cannot help but imply special creation. As Brown says, "The evolutionary tree has no trunk." [20]

"Ironically, we have even fewer examples of evolutionary transition than we had in Darwin's time."
—Geologist David Raup

This explosion of complex life is not the only way in which the fossil record condemns evolution. The lack of fossils supporting the transitional phases between species is perhaps the single most embarrassing topic for evolutionists. And yet, this absence of transitional fossils is undeniable.

This fact is grudgingly recognized by leading evolutionists. David Raup, a geologist, admits, "The record of evolution is still surprisingly jerky and, ironically, we have even fewer examples of evolutionary transition than we had in Darwin's time."[21] The problem for evolutionists unable to produce transitional fossils is made clear by Brown: "If [Darwinian] evolution happened, the fossil record should show continuous and gradual changes from the bottom to the top layers and between all forms of life. Actually, many gaps and discontinu-

Charles Darwin (1809-1882) was awarded his bachelor's degree in theology by Cambridge University in 1831. That same year, he began a five year circumnavigation of the globe as a naturalist on the *H.M.S. Beagle.* During his voyage, he studied a vast array of organisms and their habitats and began to formulate a theory about the mechanism which caused species to evolve. Eventually, he described this process as "natural selection." In 1859, he published *On the Origin of Species by Means of Natural Selection, or the Preservation of Favoured Races in the Struggle for Life.* He wrestled with his ideas until his death, ultimately producing six different editions of his landmark work.

ities appear throughout the fossil record."[22] An evolutionary tree with no trunk (no life forms earlier than the already very complex ones in Cambrian rocks) and no branches (no transitional forms) can hardly be called a tree at all.

"If a limb were to evolve into a wing, it would become a bad limb long before it became a good wing."
—WALTER T. BROWN

This problem presented by the lack of transitional forms in the fossil record also extends to the lack of transitional forms observable in nature or even conceivable in the human mind. Evolutionists are unable not only to point to a specific form observed by science as an indisputable transitional form, but also to present a reasonable explanation for the survival of any hypothetical transitional forms in nature, since many forms would be useless until fully developed.

Evolution demands that mutations be beneficial to cause them to be reproduced and become dominant in nature, and yet half-developed transitional forms provide no clear advantage. On the contrary, they are more likely to be handicaps. Brown elaborates: "If a limb were to evolve into a wing, it would become a bad limb long before it became a good wing." [23] Again, beneath the current of debate, we find the teleological argument to be among the best answers to evolutionists and the strongest support for creationism. It is clear that God as Designer provides a much better explanation for the design evidenced by life than does a theory that requires transitional forms guided by natural selection.

The fossil record, the observation of living organisms, and the teleological nature of numerous forms testify to the impossibility of gradual change. Yet gradual change is absolutely critical to traditional evolutionary theory. Darwin himself admits, "If it could be demonstrated that any complex organ existed, which could not possibly have been formed by numerous, successive, slight modifications, my theory would absolutely break down." [24]

This is precisely what creationists have claimed for years—that Darwin's evolutionary theory is bankrupt. Reason requires the biologist to abandon evolution and embrace the more rational explanation: creation. Of course, creationism is untenable for all atheists. Therefore, even if atheists recognize the irrationality of traditional evolutionary theory, they must postulate an equally indefensible theory to circumvent the notion of God.

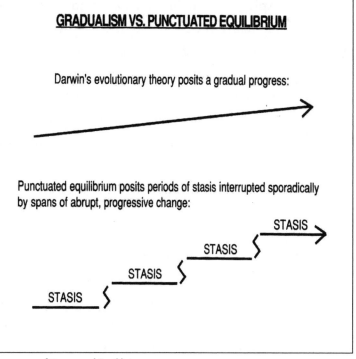

The process of Punctuated Equilibrium

PUNCTUATED EQUILIBRIUM

Thus, evolutionists recently have suggested the theory of punctuated equilibrium. This theory allows the materialistic evolutionist to escape some of the inconsistencies of neo-Darwinian evolution while ignoring the possibility of the existence of God.

Punctuated equilibrium claims that evolution occurs in spurts, in relatively short periods of time, which supposedly accounts for the absence of transitional forms. Stephen Jay Gould is the theory's leading proponent, largely because he recognizes the untenability of any evolutionary theory that requires gradual, intermediate change, but is still unwilling to abandon the theory of evolution. This forces him to postulate an alternative evolutionary theory custom-built to fit the facts.

Unfortunately for evolutionists, this approach still faces severe problems. Punctuated equilibrium continues to rely on the Darwinian mechanisms of natural selection and survival of the fittest but at a much faster pace than Darwin would allow and in isolated segments of a species' population. The problem with explaining punctuated equilibrium based on Darwinian mechanisms (even if the mechanisms were viable) is that Darwin explicitly declared that they must work gradually, imperceptibly, not rapidly and obviously.

The biggest problem with punctuated equilibrium, however, is that it is not based on evidence. Instead, it is assumed to be the correct explanation because it fits the lack of empirical evidence. But this is an illogical assumption—the lack of evidence for one proposed method of evolution does not necessarily prove the veracity of another proposed method. It might, instead, be interpreted as evidence that evolution simply did not occur.

An origins theory that cannot postulate a satisfactory mechanism but rather is based on the absence of evidence is no better than its parent theory, neo-Darwinism. Further, the speculations of punctuated equilibrium may avoid the problem of transitional forms, but they still are faced with the insurmountable problems presented by spontaneous generation, the lack of observed beneficial mutations, and evolution's contradiction of the Second Law of Thermodynamics. Punctuated equilibrium, then, is every bit as faulty as traditional evolutionary theory.

Creationism proves to be a much better explanation of man's origin, when one takes into account evidences of intelligent design throughout the universe, the complexity and ingenuity of DNA, the fossil record showing no transitional forms but rather "kind begetting kind," the extinction of species rather than new species evolving through natural selection or punctuated equilibrium, the law of biogenesis, and the Second Law of Thermodynamics.

CONCLUSION

Evolutionary theory has come full circle—from an assumption of the gradual appearance of all species to an assumption of the virtually instantaneous (geologically speaking) appearance of all species. From the Christian biologist's perspective, this is an interesting turn of events. It suggests that the evolutionists' faith in evolution is so unshakable they are willing to believe any theory that they can twist to fit the "facts" (or absence of facts).

The belief that God created all things, including man in His own image, requires faith. But evolutionary theory requires more faith, since evolution runs contrary to reason, science and history. Still, many evolutionists hold desperately to their theory, simply because it is the only explanation of origins that excludes God. The scientist who believes that everything can be explained in natural terms cannot tolerate the concept of a supernatural Being. But for the Christian biologist, the world is only comprehensible in light of God's existence.

> Evolution runs contrary to reason, science and history.

Ironically, it was Darwin's wife who eloquently verbalized the creationists' remonstrance to evolutionists. In a letter to her husband, she wrote, "May not the habit in scientific pursuits of believing nothing till it is proved, influence your mind too much in other things which cannot be proved in the same way, and which if true, are likely to be above our comprehension?"[25]

RECOMMENDED READING FOR ADVANCED STUDY:
BIOLOGY

Behe, Michael J., *Darwin's Black Box: The Biochemical Challenge to Evolution*. New York: The Free Press, 1996.

Dembski, William A. *Intelligent Design: The Bridge Between Science and Theology*. Downers Grove, Ill.: InterVarsity Press, 1999.

Denton, Michael. *Evolution: A Theory in Crisis: New Developments in Science Are Challenging Orthodox Darwinism*. Bethesda, Md.: Adler and Adler, 1996.

Moreland, J. P. *Christianity and the Nature of Science: A Philosophical Investigation*. Grand Rapids, Mich.: Baker Book House, 1989.

Morris, Henry M. *The Biblical Basis for Modern Science*. Grand Rapids, Mich.: Baker Book House, 1984.

Pearcey, Nancy R., and Charles B. Thaxton. *The Soul of Science: Christian Faith and Natural Philosophy*. Wheaton, Ill.: Crossway Books, 1994.

Thaxton, Charles B., Walter L. Bradley, and Roger L. Olsen. *The Mystery of Life's Origin*. New York: Philosophical Library, 1984.

Wells, Jonathan. *Icons of Evolution: Science or Myth? Why Much of What We Teach About Evolution is Wrong*. Washington, DC: Regnery Publishing, 2000.

ENDNOTES

1. Australian Broadcasting Co., June 10, 1976. Cited in Morris, *The Long War Against God* (Grand Rapids, Mich.: Baker, 1990), p. 58.

2. Stanley L. Jaki, *The Road of Science and the Ways to God* (Chicago: The University of Chicago Press, 1980), p. 11.

3. Langdon Gilkey, *Maker of Heaven and Earth* (Garden City, N.Y.: Doubleday, 1959), p. 110.

4. Michael Denton, *Evolution: A Theory in Crisis* (Bethesda, Md.: Adler and Adler, 1986), p. 340.

5. Michael J. Behe, *Darwin's Black Box: The Biochemical Challenge to Evolution* (New York: The Free Press, 1996) p. 232.

6. Paul Davies, *Superforce* (New York: Simon and Schuster, 1984), p. 223.

7. Denton, *Evolution: A Theory in Crisis,* p. 250.

8. Charles Thaxton, "In Pursuit of Intelligent Causes: Some Historical Background," an unpublished essay presented at an Interdisciplinary Conference in Tacoma, Washington, June 23-26, 1988, p. 13.

9. Walter T. Brown, Jr., *In the Beginning* (Phoenix: Center for Scientific Creation, 1986), p. 6.

10. Dean Kenyon, "Going Beyond the Naturalistic Mindset in Origin-Of-Life Research," *Origins Research,* Spring/Summer 1989, p. 15.

11. Brown, In the Beginning, p. 5.

12. Jonathan Wells. *Icons of Evolution: Science or Myth? Why Much of What We Teach About Evolution is Wrong* (Washington, D.C.: Regnery Publishing, 2000), p. 8.

13. A.E. Wilder-Smith, *Man's Origin, Man's Destiny* (Wheaton, Ill.: Harold Shaw, 1968), p. 55.

14. Ibid., p. 57-8.

15. Brown, *In the Beginning,* p. 9.

16. Wilder-Smith, *Man's Origin, Man's Destiny,* p. 72.

17. Pierre Paul Grasse, *Evolution of Living Organisms: Evidence for a New Theory of Transformation* (New York: Academic Press, 1977), p. 87.

18. Edward S. Deevey, Jr., "The Reply: Letter from Birnham Wood," *Yale Review* vol. 61, p. 636.

19. Charles Darwin, *The Origin of Species,* reprint of sixth edition (London: John Murray, 1902), pp. 341-2.

20. Brown, *In the Beginning,* p. 3.

21. David Raup, "Conflicts Between Darwin and Paleontology," *Field Museum of Natural History Bulletin,* January 1979, p. 25.

22. Brown, *In the Beginning,* p. 3.

23. Ibid.

24. Charles Darwin, *The Origin of Species* (London: John Murray, facsimile printed by Harvard University Press, 1966), p. 189.

25. N. Barlow, *Autobiography of Charles Darwin* (London: Collins, 1958), pp. 235-7.

CHAPTER 5

Psychology

KEY QUESTION
What is the basic nature of man?

KEY IDEA
Man has real guilt feelings about this rebellion against God, and so he must reconcile himself with God or face unsolved personal problems.

KEY QUOTE
"The great benefit of the doctrine of sin is that it reintroduces responsibility for our own behavior...."

—Paul Vitz

SUMMARY

With its emphasis on the spiritual and its understanding of man's fallen condition (Romans 1-2), only Christianity can truly address the inner-most concerns of the individual. Christian psychology helps people get in touch with their real selves because it allows them to recognize their own sinfulness and consequently their need for a Savior. Our greatest need is not self-esteem; rather, it is the realization that we are sinners in rebellion against God. As one Christian writer put it, "We're not O.K."

Only after receiving Christ as Savior can people begin to understand their value as creations in God's image and lead triumphant lives. Rather than demanding that the individual ignore his conscience, the Christian calls for him to recognize that his guilt is real, then to face his guilt and repent. Biblical Christianity teaches moral responsibility, whereas humanism and Marxism blame individual moral failings on society or the environment.

Christian psychology appears, at first glance, to be a contradiction in terms. William Kirk Kilpatrick boldly declares, "if you're talking about Christianity, it is much truer to say that psychology and religion are competing faiths. If you seriously hold to one set of values, you will logically have to reject the other."[1]

What Kilpatrick says is true. But when he uses the term psychology, he is referring specifically to secular psychology. He can make this generalization, of course, because the secular schools of psychology (based on the work of men like Sigmund Freud, B.F. Skinner, I.P. Pavlov, Carl Rogers, Abraham Maslow, and Erich Fromm) comprise virtually all of modern psychology. However, this does not mean Christians should abandon it. Instead, Christians must bring God's truth to a deceived discipline. Psychology is the study of the soul and the mind—and no worldview other than Christianity has true insight into the spiritual and mental realm. As Kilpatrick says, "In short, although Christianity is more than a psychology, it happens to be better psychology than psychology is."[2]

> Psychology is the study of the soul and the mind, and no worldview other than Christianity has true insight into the spiritual and mental realm.

Christianity and psychology are compatible for the simple reason that the worldview of biblical Christianity contains a psychology. As Charles L. Allen aptly points out, "the very essence of religion is to adjust the mind and soul of man. . . . Healing means bringing the person into a right relationship with the physical, mental and spiritual laws of God."[3]

> Genesis 1:27 So God created man in His own image; He created him in the image of God; He created them male and female.

Man created "in the image of God" (Genesis 1:27) requires a worldview that recognizes the significance of the spiritual as well as the physical.

THE SUPERNATURAL MIND

Christianity acknowledges the existence of the supernatural, including a consciousness within man that is more than an epiphenomenon of the brain. The Bible's statements regarding body, breath of life, soul, spirit, and mind suggest a dualist ontology; that is, the view that human nature consists of two fundamental kinds of reality: physical (material or natural) and spiritual (supernatural). Christ's statement about fearing the one who could put "both soul and body" in hell (Matthew 10:28), and Paul's statement regarding body, soul, and spirit (1 Thessalonians 5:23) enforce the distinction between man's material and spiritual qualities. The Bible does not deny body; it simply says man is more than body.

Sir John Eccles, one of the world's most respected neuro-physiologists, believes dualism is the only explanation for many of the phenomena of consciousness. One of the reasons Eccles reaches this conclusion is the individual's "unity of identity." Paul Weiss explains: "[E]ven though I know I am constantly changing—all molecules are changing, everything in me is being turned over substantially—there is nevertheless my identity, my consciousness of being essentially the same that I was 20 years ago. However much I may have changed, the continuity of my identity has remained undisrupted."[4] The point, of course, is that since the physical substance of the brain is constantly changing, no unity of identity could exist if consciousness were a condition wholly dependent on the physical brain. Something more than the physical brain, something supernatural, must exist.

> The Bible does not deny body; it simply says man is more than body.

Human memory is another facet of the unity-of-identity argument that supports the existence of a supernatural mind. Arthur Custance writes, "What research has shown thus far is that there is no precise one-to-one relationship between any fragment of memory and the nerve cells in which it is supposed to be encoded."[5]

Without any concept of a supernatural mind, the humanist has difficulty explaining unity of identity and memory. Still another problem arises for the Secular Humanist and Marxist: how can the materialist position account for free will? Only a worldview that postulates something other than the environment manipulating the human physical machine can account for free will. Christian dualism provides a better foundation for psychology because it defends the integrity of the mind and human free will.

HUMAN NATURE AND SIN

A proper understanding of man's nature does not, however, end with affirming the existence of a spirit within man. The Christian position goes on to define man's nature as inherently evil because of man's decision to disobey God in the garden of Eden. This understanding of man's sinful bent is critical for understanding man's nature and mental processes.

> The Christian position goes on to define mankind's nature as inherently evil because of the decision to disobey God in the garden of Eden.

This revolt by man against God caused a dramatic, reality-shattering change in the relationship of man to the rest of existence and even to himself. This change has severe ramifications for all aspects of reality, including psychology. In fact, man's sinful nature, his desire to rebel against God and his fellow man, is the source of all psychological problems, according to the Christian view. Francis A. Schaeffer sums up: "The basic psychological problem is trying to be what we are not, and trying to carry what we cannot carry. Most of all, the basic problem is not being willing to be the creatures we are before the Creator."[6]

This view is crucial for Christian theology because it allows us to understand our tremendous need for Christ's saving power. It is crucial on a lesser level, as well, for Christian psychology. In order to properly understand human nature, the psychologist must understand that man has a natural tendency to revolt against God and His laws.

> If the Christian view of the nature of mankind is correct, then only Christianity can develop a true, meaningful, and workable psychology.

If the Christian view of man's nature is correct, then only Christianity can develop a true, meaningful, and workable psychology, since only Christianity recognizes the problem of the will in relation to God. Further, only Christianity provides a framework in which man is truly held responsible for his thoughts and actions. "The great benefit of the doctrine of sin," says Paul Vitz, "is that it reintroduces responsibility for our own behavior, responsibility for changing as well as giving meaning to our condition."[7]

Only the Christian psychologist perceives man's nature in a way that is consistent with reality and capable of speaking to man's most difficult problems. The

Christian psychologist sees man as not only physical but also spiritual, as morally responsible before God, as created in God's image, and as having rebelliously turned away from his Creator. Only Christianity is prepared to face the problem that necessarily arises out of man's nature: the existence of guilt.

GUILT: PSYCHOLOGICAL OR REAL?

Both Secular Humanists and Marxists speak only of "psychological guilt" because, for them, only society is evil—people do nothing individually that would incur actual guilt. For the Christian, however, each time a man rebels against God

---

Francis Schaeffer (1912-1984)

1934 Marries Edith Seville
1938 Ordained a Presbyterian minister
1948 Begins serving as a missionary in Switzerland
1955 Establishes the Christian community L'Abri Fellowship
1976 Publishes *How Should We Then Live?*
1981 Publishes *A Christian Manifesto*

---

he is committing a sin, and the feeling of guilt that results from this rebellion is entirely justified. "Psychological guilt is actual and cruel," writes Schaeffer. "But Christians know that there is also real guilt, moral guilt before a holy God. It is not a matter only of psychological guilt; that is the distinction." [8] Because only Christian psychology acknowledges the existence of real, objective guilt, only it can speak to a person who is experiencing such guilt. As Schaeffer says, "When a man is broken in these [moral and psychological] areas, he is confused, because he has the feelings of real guilt within himself, and yet he is told by modern thinkers that these are only guilt 'feelings.' But he can never resolve these feelings, because . . . [he] has true

> While other schools of psychology must invent fancy terms to explain away the existence of real guilt as a result of real sin, Christian psychology deals with the problem at its roots.

moral awareness and the feeling of true guilt. You can tell him a million times that there is no true guilt, but he still knows there is true guilt."[9]

Christianity understands man's nature, including why this guilt arises and how to deal with it. While other schools of psychology must invent fancy terms to explain away the existence of real guilt as a result of real sin, Christian psychology deals with the problem at its roots.

MENTAL ILLNESS

Modern secular psychologists often speak of "mental illness." Yet many Christian psychologists deny the existence of a large proportion of mental illnesses. Jay Adams writes, "Organic malfunctions affecting the brain that are caused by brain damage, tumors, gene inheritance, glandular or chemical disorders, validly may be termed mental illnesses. But at the same time a vast number of other human problems have been classified as mental illnesses for which there is no evidence that they have been engendered by disease or illness at all."[10]

> *"An appreciation of the reality of sin is a critically necessary beginning point for an understanding of the Christian view of anything."*
>
> —LAWRENCE CRABB, JR.

Why is Adams so suspicious of problems that cannot be directly linked to organic causes being termed "mental illness"? "The fundamental bent of fallen human nature is away from God. . . . Apart from organically generated difficulties, the 'mentally ill' are really *people with unsolved personal problems.*"[11]

This view follows logically from the Christian perception of human nature: man has rebelled against God; he has real guilt feelings about this rebellion, and so he must reconcile himself with God or face unsolved personal problems. Lawrence Crabb, Jr. writes, "An appreciation of the reality of sin is a critically necessary beginning point for an understanding of the Christian view of anything. A psychology worthy of the adjective 'Christian' must not set the problem of sin in parallel line with other problems or redefine it into a neurosis or psychological kink."[12]

THE REALISTIC APPROACH TO SIN AND GUILT

If the Christian psychologist denies the existence of most mental illnesses, what good is his psychology? That is, how can the Christian psychologist propose to help people if he views their mental problems as spiritual problems caused by alienation from God? Doesn't this view just place too much guilt on people and avoid any real therapy?

If by the word "therapy" one means consciousness-raising seminars or primal scream workshops, then it is true the Christian psychologist does away with therapy. However, the Christian psychologist still offers solutions for the troubled person.

Because man has a conscience, and because he rebelled and continues to rebel against God, he is bound to experience real guilt. This guilt is acknowledged by the Christian psychologist, who points the hurting person toward Christ's sacrificial death and resurrection, so that the guilty can know deliverance from his guilt. Our sins will dog us daily—unceasingly—until they are washed away by Christ's shed blood.

> *James 5:16 Therefore, confess your sins to one another and pray for one another, so that you may be healed. The intense prayer of the righteous is very powerful.*

The Christian psychologist, then, must stress personal moral responsibility. Without this responsibility, the individual may deny any real guilt caused by his sins and thereby avoid the heart of his problem—his alienation from God. Only through recognizing one's sinful nature and guilt before God can anyone reconcile his guilt feelings with reality.

This may seem like a rather insensitive approach to helping people with very sensitive problems. But what could be more cruel than treating just a symptom of the problem and ignoring the actual sickness? Who would fault a doctor for giving his patient a shot to fight a disease rather than a cough drop to mask a symptom? As Adams puts it, "It is important for counselors to remember that whenever clients camouflage, . . . sick treatment only makes them worse. To act as if they may be excused for their condition is the most unkind thing one can do. Such an approach only compounds the problem." [13]

The first step for the Christian psychologist in dealing with many mental and spiritual problems is to hold each client personally responsible for the sin in his life. Crabb writes, "Hold your client responsible: for what? For confessing his sin, for willfully and firmly turning from it, and then for practicing the new behavior, believing that the indwelling Spirit will provide all the needed strength." [14]

This is the key for all Christian healing of "mental illnesses" that are not organically caused: confession of sin, forgiveness of sin through Christ (1 John 1:9), reconciliation with God (2 Corinthians 5:17-21), and sanctification through the disciplining work of God's Spirit (1 Thessalonians 5:23; Hebrews 12:1-11). Christian psychology, for all its fascination with human nature and the existence of guilt, leads to one simple method, summarized in James 5:16: "Therefore confess your sins to one another and pray for one another, so that you may be healed. The intense prayer of the righteous is very powerful."

Hebrews 12:11 No discipline seems enjoyable at the time, but painful. Later on, however, it yields the fruit of peace and righteousness to those who have been trained by it.

THE PROBLEM OF SUFFERING

Most secular psychologies attempt to alleviate all suffering for the individual. Psychologists speak of methods of "successful living" that are supposed to eradicate most pain and anguish. Vitz says this "selfist" psychology "trivializes life by claiming that suffering (and by implication even death) is without intrinsic meaning. Suffering is seen as some sort of absurdity, usually a man-made mistake which could have been avoided by the use of knowledge to gain control of the environment."[15]

> **Finding meaning in suffering is a feature unique to Christian psychology.**

In contrast, Christian psychology believes that God can use suffering to bring about positive changes in the individual. This difference between "secular" and Christian psychology has serious implications. For the non-Christian, suffering is a harsh reality that must be avoided at all cost; for the Christian, suffering may be used by God to discipline, but also to teach us many valuable lessons (Hebrews 12:7-11)—indeed, Christians are sometimes called to plunge joyously into suffering in obedience to God (Acts 6:8-7:60).

Finding meaning in suffering is a feature unique to Christian psychology. Thus we find Kilpatrick concluding, "The real test of a theory or way of life, however, is not whether it can relieve pain but what it says about the pain it cannot relieve. And this is where, I believe, psychology lets us down and Christianity supports us, for in psychology suffering has no meaning, while in Christianity it has great meaning."[16]

SOCIETY AND THE INDIVIDUAL

Christian psychology's view of human nature grants the individual moral responsibility, works to reconcile the individual with God, and gives meaning to suffering. An offshoot of this perspective is that the Christian views society as the result of individuals' actions—that is, individuals are understood to be responsible for the evils in society. This view is in direct contradiction to the Marxist and humanist view that man is corrupted by evil societies.

"Either we trust God or we take the serpent's word that we can make ourselves into gods."
—WILLIAM KIRK KILPATRICK

As always, these opposing views have logical consequences. For Marxists and humanists, society must be changed, and then man can "learn" to do right. For the Christian, however, the individual must change for the better before society can. For the Christian, blaming individual sins on society is a cop-out. As Karl Menninger says, "If a group of people can be made to share the responsibility for what would be a sin if an individual did it, the load of guilt rapidly lifts from the shoulders of all concerned. Others may accuse, but the guilt shared by the many evaporates for the individual. Time passes. Memories fade. Perhaps there is a record, somewhere; but who reads it?"[17]

The Christian, of course, knows there is a record somewhere, and is uncomfortably aware that Someone reads it. A day will come when no one can blame his sins on society. It is the duty of Christian psychologists, then, to realize the importance of personal responsibility and to impart this realization to anyone they counsel.

CONCLUSION

The Christian view of human nature is complex; ironically, it logically leads to a simple method for counseling people. Further, it is possible that Christians who properly understand human nature may never need to seek professional counseling—they may maintain spiritual well-being by remaining in submission to Christ. Schaeffer outlines a simple approach to "positive psychological hygiene": "As a Christian, instead of putting myself in practice at the center of the universe, I must do something else. This is not only right, and the failure to do so is not only sin, but it is important for me personally in this life. I must think after God, and I must will after God."[18]

The choice between Christian psychology and all other psychological schools is clear-cut. As Kilpatrick says, "Our choice . . . is really the same choice offered to Adam and Eve: either we trust God or we take the serpent's word that we can make ourselves into gods." [19]

RECOMMENDED READING FOR ADVANCED STUDY: PSYCHOLOGY

Kilpatrick, William Kirk. *Psychological Seduction.* Nashville: Thomas Nelson, 1983.

Moreland, J. P., and Scott B. Rae. *Body and Soul: Human Nature and the Crisis in Ethics.* Downers Grove, Ill.: InterVarsity Press, 2000.

Vitz, Paul C. *Psychology As Religion: The Cult of Self-Worship.* Grand Rapids, Mich.: Eerdmans, 1994.

Vitz, Paul C. *Faith of the Fatherless: The Psychology of Atheism.* Dallas: Spence Publishing, 1999.

ENDNOTES

1. William Kirk Kilpatrick, *Psychological Seduction* (Nashville: Thomas Nelson, 1983), p. 14.

2. Ibid., p. 15-6.

3. Charles L. Allen, *God's Psychiatry* (Westwood, N.J.: Revell, 1953), p. 7.

4. Paul Weiss, in *Beyond Reductionism,* eds. Koestler and Smythies, p. 251-2.

5. Arthur C. Custance, *Man in Adam and in Christ* (Grand Rapids, Mich.: Zondervan, 1975), p. 256.

6. Francis A. Schaeffer, "True Spirituality," in *The Complete Works of Francis Schaeffer,* five volumes (Westchester, Ill.: Crossway Books, 1982), vol. 3, p. 329.

7. Paul Vitz, *Psychology as Religion* (Grand Rapids Mich.: Eerdmans, 1985), p. 43.

8. Schaeffer, "True Spirituality," p. 322.

9. Ibid.

10. Jay E. Adams, *Competent to Counsel* (Grand Rapids, Mich.: Baker Book House, 1970), p. 28.

11. Ibid., p. 29.

12. Lawrence Crabb, Jr., *Basic Principles of Biblical Counseling* (Grand Rapids, Mich.: Zondervan, 1975), p. 48-9.

13. Adams, *Competent to Counsel,* p. 32-3.

14. Crabb, *Basic Principles of Biblical Counseling,* p. 44.

15. Vitz, *Psychology as Religion,* p. 103.

16. Kilpatrick, *Psychological Seduction,* p. 181.

17. Karl Menninger, *Whatever Became of Sin?* (New York: Hawthorn Books, 1974), p. 95.

18. Schaeffer, *True Spirituality,* p. 334.

19. Kilpatrick, *Psychological Seduction,* p. 233.

CHAPTER 6

Ethics

KEY QUESTION

What is right?

KEY IDEA

There must be an absolute if there is to be a
moral order and real values.

KEY QUOTE

"The human mind has no more power of inventing a new value than of imagining a new primary
colour, or, indeed, of creating a new sun and a new
sky for it to move in."

—C.S. LEWIS

SUMMARY

God's moral nature is absolute and unchanging. God always hates evil and loves good. The Bible is of supreme importance because it tells us the difference between the two, providing a framework on which a completely unambiguous ethic must be built. According to biblical Christianity, ethical relativism leads to destruction (Matthew 7:13).

Christian ethics is inseparable from theology for the simple reason that Christian ethics is grounded in the character of God. Rather than believing in some ethical scheme bound to society's ever-changing whims, the Christian answers to a specific moral order revealed to man through general revelation, the special revelation of the Bible and the person of Jesus Christ.

Christian ethics is inseparable from theology because Christian ethics is grounded in the character of God. "One of the distinctions of the Judeo-Christian God," says Francis Schaeffer, "is that not all things are the same to Him. That at first may sound rather trivial, but in reality it is one of the most profound things one can say about the Judeo-Christian God. He exists; He has a character, and not all things are the same to Him. Some things conform to His character, and some are opposed to His character."[1] The task of Christian ethics is determining what conforms to God's character and what does not.

> Christian ethics is inseparable from theology because Christian ethics is grounded in the character of God.

While Marxists and humanists rely almost exclusively on their economic or naturalistic philosophy to determine ethics, the Christian places ethics in a moral order revealed by the Divine Creator. Rather than believing in some passing fancy bound to society's ever-changing whims, the Christian answers to a specific moral order revealed to man both through general and special revelation.

The Christian knows this ethical order to be the only true source of morality. "The human mind," says C.S. Lewis, "has no more power of inventing a new value than of imagining a new primary colour or, indeed, of creating a new sun and a new sky for it to move in."[2] Those talking about establishing a new moral order are talking nonsense. This is no more possible than establishing a new physical order. Both are givens. For the Christian, the moral order is as real as the physical order—some would say more real. The Apostle Paul says the physical order is temporary, but the order "unseen" is eternal (2 Corinthians 4:18). This eternal moral order is a reflection of the character of God.

> 2 Corinthians 4:18 So we do not focus on what is seen, but on what is unseen; for what is seen is temporary, but what is unseen is eternal.

REVELATION AND OUR COMMON MORAL HERITAGE

Christian ethics in one sense is simply an expansion on a moral order that is generally revealed to all men. Despite some disputes regarding the morality of certain specific actions, comments Calvin D. Linton, "there is a basic pattern of similarity among [ethical codes]. Such things as murder, lying, adultery, cowardice are, for example, almost always condemned. The universality of the ethical sense itself (the 'oughtness' of conduct), and the similarities within the codes of diverse cultures indicate a common moral heritage for all mankind which materialism or naturalism cannot explain."[3]

> Mankind's common moral heritage could be defined as anything from an attitude to a conscience, but however one defines it, one is left with the impression that some moral absolutes exist outside of man.

This common moral heritage could be defined as anything from an attitude to a conscience, but however one defines it, one is left with the impression that some moral absolutes exist outside of man. According to this concept, whenever man judges he is relying upon a yardstick that measures actions against an absolute set of standards. Without a standard, there could be no justice; without an ethical absolute, there could be no morality.

This absolute standard outside of man is apparent through all of mankind's attitudes toward morality. Secular man should, according to his own philosophy, lead a life that treats all morals as relative—but in practice, secular man treats some abstract values (such as justice or fairness, love, and courage) as consistently moral. What's more, secular man has cringed at Auschwitz and the gulags, at child abuse and lies. How can this phenomenon be explained unless we accept the notion that certain value judgments are universal and inherent to all mankind?

Christian morality is founded on this belief that an absolute moral order exists outside of, and yet somehow inscribed into, man's very being. It is a morality flowing from the nature of the Creator through the nature of created things, not a construction of the human mind. It is part of God's general revelation to man.

> John 1:9 The true light, who gives light to everyone, was coming into the world.

This rule of right, this moral light, is what the Apostle John refers to as having been lit in the hearts of all men and women: "The true light, who gives light to everyone, was coming into the world." (John 1:9). It is what St. Paul referred to as work of the law "written on their hearts" (Romans 2:15).

This morality is not arbitrarily handed down by God to create difficulties for people. God does not make up new values according to whim. Rather, God's very character is holy and cannot tolerate evil or moral indifference—what the Bible calls sin. Therefore, if we wish to please God, we must act in accordance with His moral order so as to prevent sin from separating us from Him.

> Special revelation reveals the specifics of the moral order.

Christians are assured of these truths about God's nature and judgment as a result of special revelation. Whereas general revelation has informed all of mankind of the existence of a moral order, special revelation—the Bible—reveals specifics regarding such an order. Christian ethics, in the final analysis, relies on God and His Word for the full explanation of the moral order.

THE CHRISTIAN RESPONSE TO SECULAR ETHICS

It is important for the Christian to be able to recognize secular ideas regarding ethics and the flaws inherent in these ideas. For the Christian, morality is a lifestyle for glorifying God, and to maintain good moral health, it is crucial to stay away from the hazy thinking that suggests less-than-absolute moral values. The so-called "new morality" is nothing but an excuse to use "morality" to do as one pleases. People should have learned from history that the consequences of such a morality is death. Instead, thousands today are dying as a direct consequence of their immoral behavior.

> The so-called "new morality" is nothing but an excuse to use "morality" to do as one pleases.

Secular moralities fall back on believing that human ideas about morality are enough for an ethical code. This leaves people without a standard for judging actions with regard to morality. Schaeffer insists that there must be an absolute if there is to be a moral order and real values. "If there is no absolute beyond man's ideas, then there is no final appeal to judge between individuals and groups whose moral judgments conflict. We are merely left with conflicting opinions."[4]

This is the Achilles' heel of ethical relativism—it leaves mankind with no standards, only conflicting opinions or subjective value judgments that do not translate into real morality. The ethical vacuum created by relativism allows leaders to misuse their power without having to answer to a specific moral code. "Those who stand outside all judgments of value cannot have any ground for preferring one of their own impulses to another except the emotional strength of that impulse,"[5] writes Lewis.

For the Christian, God is the ultimate source of morality, and it is nothing short of blasphemy when we place ourselves in His role. And yet, if one does not submit to the moral absolutes founded in God's character, logically the only ethical authority over mankind is our own impulses. It is important for Christians to understand the fallacies of secular ethics, so that they can avoid the inconsistencies of unfounded ethical ideals. All secular ethical codes are an aberration of God's code and should be recognized as such.

CHRISTIAN ETHICS AND SPECIAL REVELATION

Christians emphatically embrace the concept of moral absolutes and believe they should be taught to our children. But what specific absolutes make up the moral order professed in Christian ethics? What ought we to do? How should we live?

Absolutes are revealed in the Bible. While it is impossible for every specific situation requiring moral decisions to be included in the Bible, the Christian is

---

The Ten Commandments (from Exodus 20, King James Version)
1. Thou shalt have no other gods before me.
2. Thou shalt not make unto thee any graven image.
3. Thou shalt not take the name of the Lord thy God in vain.
4. Remember the sabbath day, to keep it holy.
5. Honour thy father and thy mother.
6. Thou shalt not kill.
7. Thou shalt not commit adultery.
8. Thou shalt not steal.
9. Thou shalt not bear false witness against thy neighbour.
10. Thou shalt not covet thy neighbor's house, thou shalt not covet thy neighbour's wife, nor his manservant, nor his maidservant, nor his ox, nor his ass, nor any thing that is thy neighbour's.

---

given enough specific values and guidelines to have a sense of what is right and what is wrong in all situations. The most obvious absolutes, of course, are the Ten Commandments—the Decalogue. This acts as the "basic law" for mankind, but it is not the only law revealed in the Bible. Much of the Old Testament is dedicated to describing God's moral order.

Absolutes are revealed in the Bible.

After outlining the moral order, the Bible introduces us to God Incarnate, Jesus Christ, and describes His ministry and teachings so that Christians might better understand the implications of this order. The apex of Christ's ethical teaching is encapsulated in the Sermon on the Mount, found most comprehensively in Matthew 5-7.

For the Christian, the ethical exhortations in the Sermon on the Mount,

---

Dietrich Bonhoeffer (1906-1945) provides an inspiring example of the courage of a man committed to God. A Christian pastor in Germany, Bonhoeffer recognized the inherent evil of Nazism from its inception. When Adolf Hilter gained power in1933, Bonhoeffer helped organize the Pastors' Emergency League, a key force in the resistance movement. Believing that his faith demanded radical action, he became involved in a plot to assassinate Hitler. In 1943, he was arrested for his anti-Nazi activities, spending the last two years of his life in prison camps. His foremost writings include *Letters and Papers from Prison, The Cost of Discipleship,* and *Ethics.* On April 8, 1945, the day before he was hanged, Bonhoeffer sent a message to a friend: "This is the end, but for me, it is the beginning."

---

coupled with the ethical pronouncements of the Old Testament, create a very specific ethical order. And, as if this code were not enough, Christians have the perfect role model to dictate the proper moral course of action: Jesus Christ, as revealed in the Bible. W.E.H. Lecky, who never claimed to be a Christian, admitted, "The character of Jesus has not only been the highest pattern of virtue, but the strongest incentive to its practice. . . ."[6]

In fact, the call to follow Jesus is the simplest summation of Christian ethics, and at the same time, the most difficult thing for anyone to do. Dietrich Bonhoeffer, a twentieth-century Christian martyr, notes, "On two separate occasions Peter received the call, 'Follow me.' It was the first and last word Jesus spoke to his disciple (Mark 1:17, John 21:22)."[7] Christ really asks but one thing of Christians: Follow Me!

As a result of the special revelation given in the Bible, people can never be excused for doing wrong by claiming they have not been told what is morally correct. Throughout the Bible, the question of ethics is specifically addressed: in truth, it cannot be separated from the Christian faith.

RESPONSIBILITY IN CHRISTIAN ETHICS

Christians are called to "love the Lord your God with all your heart, with all your soul, with all your strength and with all your mind; and your neighbor as yourself" (Luke 10:27). This command, like all commands in the Bible, implies that Christians have responsibilities.

This responsibility to love others calls for an attitude not merely compassionate but servantlike. If we love God, we demonstrate it through serving our fellow human beings. It is our duty. "The Apostle John," says Carl F.H. Henry, "appeals to the explicit teaching of the Redeemer to show the inseparable connection between love of God and love of neighbor: 'If a man say, I love God, and hateth his brother, he is a liar: for he that loveth not his brother whom he hath seen, how can he love God whom he hath not seen? And this commandment have we from him, that he who loveth God love his brother also' (1 John 4:20f). 'God is love, and he that dwelleth in love dwelleth in God, and God in him' (4:16). The love of God is the service of man in love."[8]

This duty toward our fellow man requires more than serving his spiritual needs. "[M]an is more than a soul destined for another world," says Norman Geisler, "he is also a body living in this world. And as a resident of this time-space continuum man has physical and social needs which cannot be isolated from spiritual needs. Hence, in order to love man as he is—the whole man—one must exercise a concern about his social needs as well as his spiritual needs.[9]

Christians cannot claim that faith in God and the resulting perspective on life and ethics exempt them from concerns about worldly matters. Just the opposite is true (Matthew 25:31-46), because anyone who is a Christian must be concerned with working to achieve God's will for the world. God commands it.

In examining the Christian's obligation to love his neighbor, one encounters an even more fundamental obligation: the Christian's duty to love God. "The moral end, or highest good, is the glory of God," writes William Young. "In declaring by word and deed the perfections, especially the moral perfections of the most High, man finds true happiness."[10] Our duty toward God is inextricably tied to our other duties as Christians. It is accurate to state, as Henry does, "Hebrew-Christian ethics unequivocally defines moral obligation as man's duty to God."[11] This is the heart and soul of the Christian ethic.

THE INEVITABILITY OF SIN

The Bible does not concern itself only with outlining the moral order, however. It also speaks of a time when God will judge people for their character and conduct. Revelation 22:11-15 warns that at that time many will be left outside the city of God. This has staggering implications for humanity. Henry explains:

> **Christianity declares that God is more than the ground and goal of the moral order. Unequivocally it lays stress on the reality of God's judgment of history. It affirms, that is, the stark fact of moral disorder and rebellion: "the whole world lieth in wickedness." (1 John 5:19). By emphasis on the fact of sin and the shattered moral law of God, on the dread significance of death, on the wiles of Satan and the hosts of darkness, Christian ethics sheds light on the treacherous realities of moral decision.[12]**

The reality, of course, is that we "all have sinned and fall short of the glory of God" (Romans 3:23). This is a unique aspect of the Christian ethical system. "When a person makes up his own ethical code," D. James Kennedy says, "he always makes up an ethical system which he thinks he has kept. In the law of God, we find a law which smashes our self-righteousness, eliminates all trust in our own goodness, and convinces us that we are sinners. The law of God leaves us with our hands over our mouths

> "When a person makes up his own ethical code, he always makes up an ethical system which he thinks he has kept."
> —D. JAMES KENNEDY

and our faces in the dust. We are humbled before God and convinced that we are guilty transgressors of his law." [13]

This conviction of guilt is crucial for a Christian to understand the incredible sacrifice God made when He sent His Son to die for us. The Christian ethical code calls for perfection, and no one other than Christ has ever achieved that. Thus, it is the ethical code itself that points man first to his own sinful nature and then to the realization that the only One who can save him is the Man who has not stepped outside the moral code, Jesus Christ. The absolute moral code shows us our absolute dependence on Him. Put more simply, "The law is given to convince us that we fail to keep it." [14] And on realization of this truth, we are driven for salvation to the One who has not failed.

> *"It will never be lawful simply to 'be ourselves' until 'ourselves' have become sons of God."*
>
> —C.S. LEWIS

The Christian cannot, however, simply rely on Christ to save him, and then continue in his sinful ways. Rather, once the Christian understands the ultimate sacrifice God made for him, he cannot help but respond with a grateful desire to please God by adhering to His moral order. This does not mean it becomes easier for Christians to do what is morally right. It simply means that they are willing to strive to do God's will. This willingness to choose the morally right action is crucial for Christians truly concerned with pleasing God. As Lewis says, "There is nowhere this side of heaven where one can safely lay the reins on the horse's neck. It will never be lawful simply to 'be ourselves' until 'ourselves' have become sons of God." [15] Christian ethics requires a firm commitment to and an unflagging zeal for what is right and good in the Lord's sight. As Paul said, Christians must "Detest evil; cling to what is good" (Romans 12:9).

CONCLUSION

The Christian ethical system is both like and unlike any other system ever postulated. Every ethical system contains some grain of the truth found in the Christian code, but no other system can claim to be the whole truth, handed down as an absolute from God to man.

Christians, the very people who recognize this truth, must be dedicated not just to espousing it, but also to living it. This dedication has become far too rare

Clive Staples Lewis (1898-1963)
1925 Begins teaching at Magdalen College in Oxford University
1931 Converts to Christianity
1941 Delivers first series of lectures for the BBC
1942 Publishes *The Screwtape Letters*
1950 Publishes first book in the Narnia series (completed in 1956)
1952 Publishes *Mere Christianity*
1956 Marries Joy Davidman Gresham
1960 Joy dies of cancer

in present-day society. "Who stands fast?" asks Bonhoeffer. "Only the man whose final standard is not his reason, his principles, his conscience, his freedom, or his virtue, but who is ready to sacrifice all this when he is called to obedient and responsible action in faith and in exclusive allegiance to God—the responsible man, who tries to make his whole life an answer to the question and call of God. Where are these responsible people?" [16]

Where are they? Wherever Christians are willing to treat God's moral order with the same respect they show His physical order; wherever God is loved with an individual's whole body, soul, spirit, mind, and strength. They may be found in the halls of government, standing firm against tyranny and slavery, or in the mission field, sacrificing everything for the sake of the gospel. More often, these people are ordinary Christian men and women living extraordinary lives, showing the world that Christ can be believed and His standards lived. It is our Christian duty to join the ranks of these morally responsible people.

RECOMMENDED READING FOR ADVANCED STUDY: ETHICS

Beckwith, Francis J., and Michael E. Bauman. *Are You Politically Correct? Debating America's Cultural Standards.* Buffalo, N.Y.: Prometheus Books, 1993.

Beckwith, Francis J., and Gregory Koukl. *Relativism: Feet Firmly Planted in Mid-Air.* Grand Rapids, Mich.: Baker Books, 1998.

Eakman, B. K. *Cloning of the American Mind: Eradicating Morality Through Education.* Lafayette, La.: Huntington House, 1998.

Jones, David Clyde. *Biblical Christian Ethics.* Grand Rapids, Mich.: Baker Book House, 1994.

Kilpatrick, William. *Why Johnny Can't Tell Right From Wrong.* New York: Simon & Schuster, 1992.

ENDNOTES

1. Cited in John Warwick Montgomery, *Human Rights and Human Dignity* (Dallas, Tex.: Probe Books, 1986), p. 113.
2. C.S. Lewis, *The Abolition of Man* (New York: Macmillan, 1973), p. 56-7.
3. Calvin D. Linton, "Sin," in *Baker's Dictionary of Christian Ethics,* ed. Carl F.H. Henry (Grand Rapids, Mich.: Baker, 1973), p. 620.
4. Francis A. Schaeffer, *How Should We Then Live?* (Old Tappan, N.J.: Fleming H. Revell, 1976), p. 145.
5. Lewis, *The Abolition of Man,* p. 78.
6. W.E.H. Lecky, *History of European Morals (from Augustus to Charlemagne),* two volumes (New York: George Braziller, 1955), vol. 2, p. 8-9.
7. Dietrich Bonhoeffer, *The Cost of Discipleship* (New York: Macmillan, 1963), p. 48.
8. Henry, *Christian Personal Ethics,* p. 221-2.
9. Geisler, *Ethics: Alternatives and Issues* (Grand Rapids, Mich.: Zondervan, 1979), p. 179.
10. William Young, "Moral Philosophy," in *Baker's Dictionary of Christian Ethics,* ed. Henry, p. 432-3.
11. Henry, *Christian Personal Ethics,* p. 209.
12. Ibid., p. 172.
13. D. James Kennedy, *Why I Believe* (Waco, Tex.: Word Books, 1980), p. 91.
14. Ibid., p. 90.
15. C.S. Lewis, *God in the Dock* (Grand Rapids, Mich.: Eerdmans, 1972), p. 286.
16. Joan Winmill Brown, ed., *The Martyred Christian* (New York: Macmillan, 1985), p. 157.

CHAPTER 7

Sociology

KEY QUESTION

How should society be structured?

KEY IDEA

The Christian sociologist believes that family, church, and state are institutions ordained by God.

KEY QUOTE

"[Man] is not a cog in a machine,
he is not a piece of theater;
he really can influence history."
—FRANCIS A. SCHAEFFER

SUMMARY

Christian sociology is based on the proposition that the individual as well as the social order are important to God, mankind and society. Christ died and rose again for each person as an individual. God also ordained social institutions to teach love, respect, discipline, work, and community. Family, church and state are the three most important of these. Christian sociology focuses both on society as a means for human cooperation with God's will, and on the individual as a vital part of the social institutions within society.

Every sociologist acknowledges the existence of certain social institutions such as family, church, and government. Sociologists differ, however, when describing the origin of these institutions and their relationship to the individual. This difference results from the assumptions inherent in the sociologist's worldview. While the Christian views mankind as specially created in God's image and pantheists understand people actually to be god, the atheistic worldviews see mankind simply as an evolving sexual animal, without soul or spirit. Man without soul or spirit is nothing more than a farm animal. Unfortunately, this latter view is the predominant perspective among humanistic sociologists. God, Adam and Eve, the garden of Eden, and the sacred character of the family are considered pre-scientific myths. Christians believe that this erroneous view is largely responsible for the many failures in modern sociology (e.g., its inability to suggest proper solutions to family deterioration, drug abuse, crime, and poverty).

Humanistic sociologists view mankind simply as an evolving sexual animal, without soul or spirit.

FREE WILL AND SOCIETY

One of the fundamental ways in which Christian sociology differs from the humanist and Marxist approaches is Christianity's affirmation of individual free will and responsibility. Atheistic approaches, when consistent with their own concepts, believe that society determines man's consciousness and actions, whereas Christianity describes man as a creature with the freedom to choose between right and wrong and to shape society.

The Christian view grants individuals much more control over society, but it also burdens them with much more responsibility. People, in the Christian perspective, must face the consequences of their decisions. This point is made painfully clear in the opening chapters of Genesis, when Adam and Eve bring a curse on the whole human race and are exiled from the garden of Eden, all because

> **People, in the Christian perspective, must face the consequences of their decisions.**

they choose to disobey God. "If man's behavior were somehow conditioned by genetic code or social externals," says William Stanmeyer, "then no just judge could blame him for the evil he commits. But the scripture teaches unequivocally that God blamed Adam and Eve for succumbing to the temptation to disobedience and punished them accordingly."[1]

The Genesis account of Adam and Eve not only demonstrates that man is responsible for his actions, but also describes another key belief for Christians: every human is guilty before God. "The fact of guilt," according to author Rousas Rushdoony "is one of the major realities of man's existence."[2]

Christian sociology attempts to understand society in light of man's free will and the consequences of his freely choosing to turn from God. The Fall caused every human society to be marked by alienation. To put it bluntly, ever since God gave people free will and the ability to create their own societies, the record has been one of degeneration and devolution, not evolution. The alienation caused

Genesis 3:6-7; 22-4 Then the woman saw that the tree was good for food, and delightful to look at, and that it was desirable for obtaining wisdom. So she took some of its fruit and ate; she also gave some to her husband, who was with her, and he ate. ⁷Then the eyes of both of them were opened, and they knew they were naked; so they sewed together fig leaves and made loincloths for themselves. . . . ²²The Lord God said, "Since man has become like one of Us knowing good and evil and must not reach out, take from the tree of life as well, eat, and live forever—" ²³ The Lord God sent him away from the garden of Eden to work the ground from which he was taken. ²⁴He drove out man, and stationed the cherubim east of the garden of Eden with the flaming, whirling sword to guard the way to the tree of life.

by human sin pervades all relationships.

Man's alienation from God, from the rest of mankind, and from himself plays a crucial role in the Christian approach to sociology. A sociologist who believes that people are alienated will interpret data differently from one who believes that they are inherently good but corrupted by society.

THE INHERENT WORTH OF THE INDIVIDUAL

It would seem, at this point, that the Christian sociologist is the most pessimistic of all sociologists, since he perceives man as consistently making the wrong decisions. In reality, however, God's saving grace makes the Christian position the most optimistic. Free will and responsibility before God grant mankind far more significance than do views based on atheism or pantheism. Man "is not a cog in a machine," says Francis A. Schaeffer, "he is not a piece of theater; he really can influence history. From the biblical viewpoint, *man is lost, but great*." [3]

> To the Christian, the individual is more important than any institution or society.

The Christian perspective sees every individual as valuable and capable of making an important contribution to society. While other sociologists view the individual as basically helpless in the face of societal pressures, the Christian sees every individual as free and therefore capable of influencing society. To the Christian, the individual is more important than any institution or society.

C.S. Lewis drives this point home by observing that atheists think "nations, classes, civilizations must be more important than individuals," because "the individuals live only seventy odd years each and the group may last for centuries. But to the Christian, individuals are more important, for they live eternally; and races, civilizations and the like, are in comparison the creatures of a day." [4]

MAN AS A SOCIAL BEING

The fact that Christians value the individual over the social order, however, does not diminish the importance of sociology in a Christian worldview. Christians understand that society plays a key role in history and in the individual's relationship with God. Above all, they recognize that man was created a social being (Genesis 2:20).

> *Genesis 2:20 The man gave names to all the livestock, to the birds of the sky, and to every wild animal; but for Adam no helping counterpart was found.*

S.D. Gaede stresses the inherent social nature of man, stating, "God designed the human being to be a relational creature. Note this point well. Humankind was created to relate to other beings. It was not an accident. It was not the result of sin. It was an intentional, creational given." [5]

Of course, mankind's relations in this life will always be hindered by feelings of alienation. Gaede refers to this problem as the "relational dilemma" and views it as truth that must be recognized by all sociologists who wish to understand society in the proper perspective. In this context, Christians recognize the true cause of alienation in society and can competently study the results and offer a solution to the world.

CHRISTIAN PLURALISM

Since Christian sociologists maintain that the individual is more important than any institution in society, society is important because man was created a social being. This sociological perspective is referred to as a pluralist view, because

People were created to enjoy relationships with each other.

the sociologist does not perceive society or the individual as the only true reality. The view that society exclusively shapes reality is called collectivism; the view that only individuals affect reality is called individualism.

Both the humanist and the Marxist approach sociology from the collectivist perspective. That is, because these worldviews hold that man is inherently good but is caused by society to either deny or embrace his goodness,

> *"Individualism is a fatal poison.
> But individuality is the salt
> of common life. You may have
> to live in a crowd, but you do
> not have to live like it, nor
> subsist on its food."*
>
> —HENRY VAN DYKE

they perceive society as creating reality and the individual as helpless and insignificant.

The proper perspective is a pluralist view of man and society. This perspective ensures that man "can never be reduced to either a mere atomistic individual or a mere integer in some social whole."[6] It also holds both man and society accountable to God (2 Kings 17:7f; Acts 17:31).

By regarding every member and aspect of society as responsible, the Christian sociologist naturally expects each institution in society to focus on governing its own realm of interests properly and to allow other institutions the same freedom.

BIBLICALLY PRESCRIBED INSTITUTIONS

Christian sociologists believe that family, church, and state are institutions ordained by God. Some Christians, such as Dietrich Bonhoeffer, would add labor to this list of God-ordained institutions. For the Christian, it is extremely significant that God ordained certain societal institutions, because this indicates the relevance of Christianity to every aspect of reality. As Bonhoeffer says, "It is God's will that there shall be labour, marriage, government, and church in the world; and it is His will that all these, each in its own way, shall be through Christ, directed towards Christ, and in Christ. . . . This means that there can be no retreating from a 'secular' into a 'spiritual' sphere."[7]

This is an important concept for Christians to grasp. After examining a list of the social institutions Christians understand to be ordained by God, one might get the impression that some aspects of society are outside the realm of Christianity. This, however, is not the case. All of society—indeed, all of life—is bound up inextricably with God and His plan for mankind. As Bonhoeffer says, "the world is relative to Christ."[8]

Acts 17:31 He has set a day on which He is going to judge the world in righteousness by the Man He has appointed. He has provided proof of this to everyone by raising Him from the dead.

In the remainder of this chapter, we will focus on the Christian view of two social institutions: the family and the church. We will examine the state later, in the politics chapter, and labor in the economics chapter.

MARRIAGE AND THE FAMILY

For the Christian, marriage and the family are ordained by God (Genesis 2:23-25) and, together, will always be the fundamental institution of society. The Christian believes that the family and its role are strictly defined in the Bible. As James Dobson and Gary Bauer say, the family exists when "husband and wife are lawfully married, are committed to each other for life, and [the family] adheres to the traditional values on which the family is based."[9]

Genesis 2:23-5 And the man said, "This one at last is bone of my bone, and flesh of my flesh: this one will be called woman, for this one was taken from man. ²⁴This is why man leaves his father and his mother and bonds with his wife and they become one flesh. ²⁵The man and his wife were both naked and felt no shame.

George Gilder believes, as do many Christian sociologists, that the condition of marriage and family in any given society describes the condition of the entire society. If the family is troubled, so is society. It is to society's advantage to build and encourage the God-ordained institution of marriage and the family.

Unfortunately, modern American society does more to discourage marriage and family than to build it up. This disdain for marriage and the family stems largely from the popularity of the Secular Humanist perspective and its brainchild, the sexual revolution. Public school children in sex education courses are being subjected to some of the most bizarre concepts and practices imaginable. Not only is homosexuality being taught as a normal lifestyle and not only are students given condoms and advised to practice their usage, but teenage girls are being instructed about obtaining abortions without parental knowledge or consent. As Dobson and Bauer note, such sex-ed programs are "a crash course in relativism, in immorality, and in anti-Christian philosophy."[10]

It is not coincidental that these attacks on the traditional family come largely from proponents of relativistic, materialistic worldviews. The humanist and the Marxist disregard the existence of the spirit and the soul and thereby devalue the

George Gilder *(1939-)* is perhaps the most popular of all American supply-side economists, as well as a leading Christian sociologist. After graduating from Harvard in 1962, he worked as a speechwriter for a number of key political figures, including Richard Nixon. In 1973, he published his first major book, *Sexual Suicide,* which he later expanded and revised as *Men and Marriage.* It remains one of the foremost apologetics for the Christian model of the family. His most popular work, *Wealth and Poverty,* was published in 1981, in which he stresses that free markets are essential to the creation of wealth.

family's importance for mankind. The Christian, however, recognizes marriage and the family as the institution that nurtures the whole individual. The family should provide an environment that encourages both mental and spiritual growth.

THE CHURCH IN SOCIETY

God ordained the church to serve specific functions. One of the principal roles of the church is the proclamation of sin and salvation. By making society aware of sin, the church can effect great positive changes. If society does not repent of its sin, it will be judged. But the church can play a critical role in turning a society toward God by explaining that both the individual and society have sinned and are responsible for their actions.

The church also can cause a society to face God by providing an example of true community. If the Christian church could show the rest of society that it is possible to live according to the command "Love your neighbor as yourself,"

The church's role is to remind both individuals and society that they have sinned and are responsible to God for their actions.

then individuals and society might be more willing to turn to God and acknowledge Him as the initiator of all relations. Schaeffer is adamant about the need for community in the Christian church: "I am convinced that in the 20th century people all over the world will not listen if we have the right doctrine, the right polity, but are not exhibiting community."[11] This sentiment, grounded in Ephesians 4:11-16, is just as true for us living in the 21st century.

CONCLUSION

Christian sociology values both the individual and society. The individual is seen as capable of free choice, though alienated because of man's decision to turn from God. Society also is seen as fallen and imperfect, as well as responsible for its decisions and attitudes. It is in this perspective that both society and the individual gain value: only people and institutions capable of choosing are truly significant. Any person or any society whose actions are determined by uncontrollable forces has no more value than a tree or a stone.

> *"Bless all the churches, and blessed be God, who, in this our great trial, giveth us the churches."*
> —ABRAHAM LINCOLN

Ephesians 4:11, 16 And He personally gave some to be apostles, some prophets, some evangelists, some pastors and teachers, . . . From Him the whole body, fitted and knit together by every supporting ligament, promotes the growth of the body for building up itself in love by the proper working of each individual part.

In this context of responsibility, the Christian recognizes that people must face the consequences for the choices they make in creating society. People are charged with the duty of protecting and directing the growth of societal institutions ordained by God, including family, state and church. The family is charged with the generational or reproductive responsibilities; the state is charged with justice issues which primarily involve maintaining law and order; the church is charged with making sure Christian love is the cement of the social institutions. People are answerable to God for the direction in which society is led by these institutions. The same burden of responsibility points us to our blessing: we are the free creatures of a loving and just God.

RECOMMENDED READING FOR ADVANCED STUDY: SOCIOLOGY

Blankenhorn, David. *Fatherless America.* New York: Basic Books, A Division of HarperCollins Publishers, 1995.

Clark, Gordon H. *A Christian Philosophy of Education.* Jefferson, Md.: The Trinity Foundation, 1988.

Dobbs, Zygmund, ed. *The Great Deceit: Social Pseudo-Sciences.* West Sayville, N.Y.: Veritas Foundation, 1964.

D'Souza, Dinesh. *Illiberal Education: The Politics of Race and Sex on Campus.* New York: The Free Press, 1991.

Reisman, Judith A. *Kinsey, Sex and Fraud.* Lafayette, La.: Huntington House Publishers, 1990.

ENDNOTES

1. William A. Stanmeyer, *Clear and Present Danger* (Ann Arbor, Mich.: Servant Books, 1983), p. 42.

2. Rousas John Rushdoony, *Politics of Guilt and Pity* (Fairfax, Va.: Thoburn Press, 1978), p. 1.

3. Francis A. Schaeffer, *Death in the City* (Downers Grove, Ill.: InterVarsity Press, 1976), p. 81.

4. C.S. Lewis, *God in the Dock* (Grand Rapids, Mich.: Eerdmans, 1972), p. 109-10.

5. S.D. Gaede, *Where Gods May Dwell* (Grand Rapids, Mich.: Zondervan, 1985), p. 98.

6. Rockne McCarthy, Donald Oppewal, Walfred Peterson, and Gordon Spykman, *Society, State, and Schools* (Grand Rapids, Mich.: Eerdmans, 1982), p. 18.

7. Dietrich Bonhoeffer, *Ethics* (New York: Macmillan 1959), p. 207.

8. Ibid.

9. James C. Dobson and Gary L. Bauer, *Children at Risk: The Battle For the Hearts and Minds of Our Kids* (Dallas, TX: Word, 1990), p. 112.

10. Ibid., p. 55. For an in-depth look at what is transpiring in such classroom instruction we recommend Dobson and Bauer's book, Phyllis Schlafly's *Child Abuse in the Classroom* (Alton, Ill., Marquette Press, 1985), and Judith A. Reisman and Edward W Eichel's *Kinsey, Sex and Fraud* (Lafayette, LA: Huntington House, 1990).

11. Francis A. Schaeffer, *The Church at the End of the 20th Century* (Downers Grove, Ill., InterVarsity Press, 1974), p. 73.

CHAPTER 8

Law

KEY QUESTION

What is the basis for law?

KEY IDEA

General and special revelation together
provide enough information for people
to implement a legal system that need not
depend on the wisdom of sinful
human beings.

KEY QUOTE

"Upon these two foundations, the law of
nature and the law of revelation
[the Bible], depend all human laws."
—WILLIAM BLACKSTONE

SUMMARY

The Christian concept of law consists of both natural and biblical law originating in the very character of a righteous and loving God. Divine law is eternal because God is eternal. It is so permanent that someday God will use it to judge the world (Acts 17:31) in a judgment based on natural and revealed law (Romans 2:12f).

God established human government and the rule of law primarily to keep in check humanity's sinful nature and passions (Romans 13:1-4). Because of the Fall, human history reflects a continuing effort by people to substitute man-made law for God's law.

Christians believe that when God's laws are obeyed, people and societies thrive. The Christian concept of human rights involves the biblical doctrine of man's creation in the image of God. These rights, which carry with them specific responsibilities, are unalienable. God's Word and nature's law are sufficient for mankind to establish a legal system that exemplifies man's creative image, but does not soft-pedal his depravity.

The Christian believes that God has provided laws (and a means of discovering those laws) for mankind. "God is the only Legislator," says Carl F.H. Henry. "Earthly rulers and legislative bodies are alike accountable to Him from whom stems all obligation—religious, ethical and civil."[1]

If this is true, it presents serious implications for all of mankind, and not only in the realm of law. This becomes obvious when one examines the assumptions

God is the ultimate Law-giver to whom all human authorities are accountable.

and consequent failings implicit in every man-centered system of law. Systems that deny God as Law-giver ultimately fail and will always adversely affect every individual mired in them. They fail because they recognize neither the dignity of man created in the image of God nor the fallen nature of man.

SYSTEMS OF MAN-CENTERED LAW

If God does exist and does create law, then any society that ignores His laws will be out of step with reality. Further, a society or state that ignores God will promote arbitrary laws, consequently causing its subjects to lose respect for the legal system. John Whitehead believes that when fundamental principles of law are undermined, "public confidence in law and public willingness to abide by law are also sapped."[2] The reason public trust disappears is simple: when law is not considered sacred, neither is it considered binding. If fallen human beings are in charge of creating law, one can rest assured that people will constantly recreate the law to better suit selfish interests—either of the law-maker or of the law-maker's own constituents. Disregard for man-made law causes the individual to adopt an arbitrary attitude toward other areas of life—most notably, ethics.

> The reason public trust disappears is simple: when law is not considered sacred, neither is it considered binding.

Without a law that is both unchanging and worthy of obedience, where can the individual discover a moral code apart from that made up by other people? People quickly realize that if God does not exist, all things are permissible.

Unfortunately, many modern states and the United Nations are based on positive law (or man-made law, often referred to as legal positivism). As predicted, this absence of a proper legal foundation is creating breakdowns throughout societies. Indeed, the bankruptcy of the modern world's legal and ethical codes powerfully demonstrates the need for a legal basis outside of that created by people alone. It is estimated that over 170 million citizens have been murdered at the hands of their own communist and fascist governments between 1917 and 1998. The total could be as high as 360 million.[3] "The horrors of our recent history," writes John Warwick Montgomery, "[have] forced us to recognize the puerile inadequacy of tying ultimate legal standards to the mores of a particular society, even if that society is our own."[4]

> People quickly realize that if God does not exist, all things are permissible.

AN ABSOLUTE STANDARD

Clearly, the weakest aspect of the theory of legal positivism is its founding of law on an ever-changing basis: governmental authority. Legal positivists believe a "flexible" system of law is desirable, since man and his laws are caught up in the process of evolution. But the failings of such a system are obvious, as A.E. Wilder-Smith points out: "Since humans are allegedly accidents, so are their laws."[5]

> *Positive law* is also known as man-made law or legal positivism.

The legal positivist would not put it quite that way. Positivists believe laws are logically formulated by the state to best suit mankind's evolutionary needs (for example, homosexuality might be legalized to avoid the hypothetical danger of over-population). However, this does not negate the fact that laws become arbitrary in such a system. Indeed, legal positivism creates a profound danger: the all-powerful state.

Society is faced with a choice: "[I]f there is no fixity in law and no reference point," writes Whitehead, "then law can be what a judge says it is. If, however, there is a fixity to law, there is some absolute basis upon which judgment can be made."[6] Society must decide whether an absolute legal standard exists. It does not matter whether society would prefer fixed or flexible laws. What matters is whether an absolute code is real. If such a code does exist, we must discover and obey it, for it points to a Law-giver worthy of our obedience and worship.

The Christian, of course, believes such laws and such a Law-giver exist. For the Christian, law is grounded on the firmest foundation and therefore does not flex or evolve. Whitehead insists that law in the Christian sense has something more than mere form. "Law has content in the eternal sense. It has a reference point. Like a ship that is anchored, law cannot stray far from its mooring."[7] The Christian perspective creates a legal system that does not fluctuate according to the whims of people who have legislative power, and therefore, it creates a system that is more just.

Moses received the Ten Commandments directly from God, the source of law.

The Christian approach to law not only provides law with an absolute foundation in God as the ultimate Law-giver but also clears up confusion over the nature of law. Whereas legal positivists can explain neither why laws must exist nor why man can never develop a just system of law, the Christian legal theorist provides a simple, logical answer: man is in rebellion against God and His law. Earthly laws are required to curb that rebellion, but the implementation of these laws will always be imperfect, since man's fallen nature keeps him from formulating and enforcing a just legal system.

But if people are truly corrupted by sin, how can they discover any of God's laws? If human nature is fallen, and people are no longer in touch with God's will, how can they know what God commands them to do? The answer lies in both general and special revelation.

NATURAL AND BIBLICAL LAW

God reveals His law to people, in general, through natural law. Every person has a conscience, an inherent sense of right and wrong. The Apostle Paul says, "So, when Gentiles, who do not have the law, instinctively do what the law demands, they are a law to themselves even though they do not have the law" (Romans 2:14). Christianity teaches that people can, to some extent, perceive the will of God, and that this perceived will is the law of nature. William Blackstone, a Christian and one of the most influential figures in the history of law, describes natural law this way: "Man, considered as a creature, must necessarily be subject to the laws of his creator, for he is an entirely dependent being. . . . And consequently as man depends absolutely upon his maker for everything, it is necessary that he should in all points conform to his maker's will. This will of his maker is called the law of nature."[8]

Romans 1:26-7 This is why God delivered them over to degrading passions. For even their females exchanged natural sexual intercourse for what is unnatural.[27] The males in the same way also left natural sexual intercourse with females and were inflamed in their lust for one another. Males committed shameless acts with males and received in their own persons the appropriate penalty for their perversion.

This view is consistent with the biblical account of Creator, creation, moral order, and law. The Apostle Paul specifically discusses the concept of natural law in Romans 1-2, claiming that all people have a fundamental knowledge that there is a transcendental law by which they should abide, and yet which they fail to obey. Fallen nature does not destroy the awareness of this general revelation. Though "we see indistinctly, as in a mirror," (1 Corinthians 13:12) we nevertheless do see.

The theory that natural law is grounded in God's general revelation is crucial to the Christian's legal perspective. Understood properly, natural law explains why all people are considered accountable to God for their actions: because all are aware of the existence of a transcendent law and still consciously disobey it.

Further, the Christian legal theorist must reckon with God's special revelation. God has made His law known to people through the Bible. Natural law provides a general concept of right and wrong, but the Bible fleshes out this skeletal frame-work so that people may know what God considers lawful. A classic example of this is found in Leviticus 18. God warns Moses about the legal structures of Egypt and Canaan—"You must not follow their statutes"—and insists that Israel not permit incest, adultery, infanticide (abortion), homosexuality, and bestiality. These practices still intrigue the natural, fallen man, but God considers them an abomination because they are contrary to nature (Romans 1:26-27) and undermine the dignity and sanctity of the God-ordained home.

> *"Our human laws are but the copies, more or less imperfect, of the eternal laws, so far as we can read them."*
>
> —J.A. FROUDE

General and special revelation together provide enough information for people to implement a legal system that need not depend merely on the wisdom of sinful human beings. Indeed, this revelation is made available to all people, regardless of their intellectual capacities. General and specific revelation provide everyone with the guidance necessary to create a reasonably just system of law. Says Blackstone, "Upon these two foundations, the law of nature and the law of revelation [the Bible], depend all human laws. . ."[9] These two foundations may be called Christian or divine law.

Divine law provides a definite means of judging laws enacted by societies. While legal positivists have no criteria for judging the appropriateness of a law other than the perceived needs of the people affected, the Christian can (and must) refer to the divine law as the basis for declaring a law just or unjust. This creates certain implications for Christian legal theory.

> Government exists not so much to create laws as to secure laws, to apply God's laws to general and specific situations.

DIVINE LAW

If God has given people a means of discovering and implementing divine law, then a true and just legal system must be based on this revealed law. Without divine law, individuals have no standard for judging any legal system imposed upon them.

Thus, government exists not so much to create laws as to secure laws, to apply God's laws to general and specific situations, and to act as the impartial enforcer of such laws. Whitehead argues that the very term "legislator" means not one who makes laws but one who moves them— moves them "from the divine law written in nature or in the Bible into the statutes and law codes of a particular society." [10]

Romans 13:3-4 For rulers are not a terror to good conduct, but to bad. Do you want to be unafraid of the authority? Do good and you will have its approval. For government is God's servant to you for good. But if you do wrong, be afraid, because it does not carry the sword for no reason. For government is God's servant, an avenger that brings wrath on the one who does wrong.

The Declaration of Independence, authored primarily by Thomas Jefferson, calls the idea of God-given rights "self-evident."

As will be demonstrated in the chapter on politics, government—according to God's plan—should concern itself with encouraging people to obey God's will and with punishing evildoers (Romans 13:3-4). Legal systems should consist of laws conforming to divine law such that wrongdoers are punished by the system while those who walk according to God's will are protected. Paul explains in 1 Timothy 1 that the righteous do not fear state law because they already obey nature's law, which is God's eternal law. The unrighteous need the law to keep them within certain boundaries of acceptable behavior, thereby protecting the innocent citizen from lawlessness.

The courts should reflect this attitude. Rather than concerning themselves with creating laws, courts must simply apply laws so that God's justice is served. In the past, this attitude was implicit within legal theory. The "fact that courts were once seen as institutions of justice (not legislating bodies) cannot be underscored enough,"[11] says Whitehead. The Christian calls for a return to this approach.

False law-making—such as "concessions to the majority" as a basis for the legalization of abortion, homosexuality, pedophilia, or incest—will not be tolerated by God. A society that consciously turns away from divine law will suffer the consequences. "The clear pattern throughout Scripture," says Montgomery, "is that those who do God's will live and those who flaunt His commands perish."[12]

It is in everyone's best interest to ground a society's legal system in divine law. Indeed, it is doubly in the best interest of all people because obedience to divine law is the only true freedom—all disobedience results in personal and/or political enslavement. This is consistent with Paul's assertion, "But now, since you have been liberated from sin and become enslaved to God, you have your fruit, which results in sanctification—and the end is eternal life!" (Romans 6:22).

Christian law consists of five basic precepts:

(1) **The source of all divine law is the character or nature of God. Says Francis A. Schaeffer, "God has a character, and His character is the law of the universe."[13] Not all things are the same to Him. Some things conform to His character, and some do not.**

(2) **The moral order proceeds out of the character of God. This order is as real as the physical order and reflects God's character—His holiness, justice, truth, love, and mercy.**

(3) **Man is created in the image of God and therefore has significance. Life is not an afterthought. God established human government to protect human life, rights and dignity (Genesis 9:6).**

(4) **When Jesus Christ took human form (John 1:14), human life took on even greater significance. God the Creator was now God the Redeemer.**

(5) **Christian law is also based on the fact that someday God through Christ will judge the whole human race (Acts 17:31; Romans 2:16) according to a standard of good**

> **and evil (2 Corinthians 5:10). Christians, realizing that they stand guilty before such an awesome God, flee to Jesus Christ for safety.**

The extent to which society and the individual acknowledge and obey divine law affects the entire fabric of their existence. Nowhere is the truth of this assertion more obvious than in the realm of human rights. As Gary Amos points out, "The biblical model of rights cannot be separated from the biblical teaching about justice."[14] A people's response to divine law creates a specific attitude about human rights.

DUTIES AND RIGHTS

The Christian calls for mankind to discover human rights in God's revealed Word, the Bible. Indeed, the Christian believes that the Bible is the only true source of rights, since it is the only special revelation of God's truth. Under this

America's founders based our system of law on the concept that rights are given by God, not the state.

system, people are more certainly guaranteed specific rights than under any other system proposed through any other worldview.

The reason is simple. If, as the Bible claims, man is created in the image of God, then each human life becomes inestimably precious and meaningful. This, in turn, creates a firm foundation on which a system of human rights can be built.

These rights are tied to Christian law much more closely than in other legal systems.

According to the Christian perspective, God commands people to obey divine law, and this obedience is what guarantees the protection of rights for everyone. God has made people responsible for upholding human rights by binding legal duties to those rights. If people live biblically, each person will possess the complete range of rights granted by God. But if people disobey God, then the system of rights revealed in the Bible will suffer.

Notice that this concept also places specific limitations on a person's rights. No one may claim, "I've got my rights!" and then act in any manner he or she pleases. Divine law requires that people continually act according to the true order of the universe, to walk in God's will. Amos provides a fine example: "Men have rights, such as the right to life. But because a man has a duty to live his life for God, the right is inalienable. He can defend his life against all others, but not destroy it himself. No man has the right to do harm to himself, to commit suicide, or to waste his life. He has a property interest—dominion—in his own life, but not total control." [15]

America's Declaration of Independence was built on just such an unchanging basis for rights. Thomas Jefferson, primary author of the Declaration, proclaimed the need for this basis when he asked rhetorically, "Can the liberties of a nation be thought secure when we have removed their only firm basis, a conviction in the minds of the people that these liberties are the gift of God?" [16]

Thomas Jefferson clearly viewed rights and liberties as gifts from God to mankind.

BIBLICAL APPLICATIONS

The Bible presents God's guidelines for an earthly system of law. God expects man to devise an ordered legal system and provides him with an example in Exodus. In this system, judges were instituted (Exodus 18:13-16; Deuteronomy 1:16-17; 19:15-21), along with a multi-tiered judicial system. "The judges were commanded to be honest and not to take bribes or favor the rich (Exodus 23:1-8)," [17] says John Eidsmoe.

From this we can conclude that God's ideal legal system is not only orderly but also equitable. Every man is granted the right to be judged according to the same standards of justice. Deuteronomy 1:17 clearly states, "Do not show partiality in legal decisions; listen to small and great alike."

The Bible has a relevant message for legal theory in the realm of assigning guilt as well. Simon Greenleaf says, "the importance of extreme care in ascertaining the truth of every criminal charge, especially where life is involved, may be regarded as a rule of law. It is found in various places in the Mosaic Code, particularly in the law respecting idolatry; which does not inflict the penalty of death until the crime 'be told thee,' (viz. in a formal accusation), 'and thou hast heard of it,' (upon a legal trial), 'and inquire diligently, and behold to be true,' (satisfactorily proved), 'and the thing certain,' (beyond all reasonable doubt)." [18]

> *"The Christian . . . sees justice as rooted in the loving will of God, a will directed towards the good of the beings he created and exemplified in his dealings with men."*
> —PETER A. DE VOS

Christian legal theory recognizes that an earthly judge should not be hasty in condemning any man. Because man is fallen and his reason exists in a less-than-perfect state, it is quite possible for man to err in dispensing justice. According to the Christian position, it is better for the earthly judge to err in favor of the defendant than to punish an innocent man, because ultimately all lawbreakers will be judged by God. Where justice might not be served by earthly courts, it will most certainly be served on the final judgment day (Acts 17:31).

Unfortunately, modern man has lost his faith in an ultimate Judge and judgment day, and many of his evil tendencies go unchecked. The Bible clearly indicates how a system of law should respond to criminal actions: not only with punishment, but with a sincere effort to restore God's order which has been disrupted by the criminal act. Biblical law requires restitution to the offended person, while also demanding the restoration of God's order.

The Christian believes it is proper to attempt to restore God's order in the world. This belief, however, should not cause the Christian to conclude that every sin should be made explicitly illegal.

IS IT POSSIBLE TO LEGISLATE MORALITY?

In one sense, law and morality are inseparable. When one declares theft illegal, one is making a moral judgment—theft is condemned as immoral, because it violates divine law.

> *"The fundamental basis of this nation's law was given to Moses on the Mount. The fundamental basis of our Bill of Rights comes from the teaching which we get from Exodus and St. Matthew, from Isaiah and St. Paul. . . . If we don't have the proper fundamental moral background, we will finally wind up with a totalitarian government which does not believe in rights for anybody except the state."*
> —HARRY S. TRUMAN, PRESIDENT OF THE UNITED STATES, 1945-52

This does not mean that all morals must be enforced by specific laws. A system making all sin illegal would, among other things, cause government to become even more bloated in an effort to enact and enforce a vast array of new laws. People must concentrate on formulating a legal system that legislates morality only to the extent that order is maintained and human rights are protected.

The task of earthly law, according to the Christian, is not to cause people always to act morally. No law could ever hope to accomplish that. And yet, if law is tied so closely to morals, it must affect people's moral nature on a deeper level than simply causing them to behave in an orderly way and to respect human rights. How, then, does law serve to bring people to a right understanding of God's universe? The answer is that no one is capable of living a completely lawful life. This inability to act morally is made obvious by the violations of God's divine law as stated in Scripture or as represented by earthly legal systems.

The equitable application of laws requires a balanced administration of justice that fairly evaluates all the pertinent facts of a particular case.

Thus, a Christian system of law, while stabilizing society and promoting justice (by protecting the weak and innocent, and by punishing the guilty), also leads individuals to the knowledge that they are fallen creatures desperately in need of a Savior. Much as general revelation points to natural law, earthly legal systems help the nonbeliever recognize the corrupt nature of every person and seek the reasons behind this corruption and the remedy for it. God in His wisdom uses law not only to ensure justice, but also to demonstrate that, in our fallen state,

> *"So many laws argue so many sins."*
>
> —JOHN MILTON

it would be folly to demand our just desserts. Rather, all should beg for mercy and turn to Christ for salvation, thereby becoming children of God (see Ephesians 2).

CONCLUSION

Christian law is based on God's unchanging character. This forms an absolute foundation for law and, in turn, shows Christianity to be better equipped to offer a system of law than all the worldviews that call for an evolutionary legal system. Christian law supports specific, absolute human rights that cannot be ensured by worldviews which deny God's existence. Christian human rights are based on

Christian law is based on God's unchanging character.

specific duties prescribed in the Bible—thus, God assigns specific rights to all humans, but people become responsible for obeying God and protecting those rights for themselves and for others.

God makes specific provisions in the Bible for earthly legal systems. He expects them to be both orderly and equitable. God further expects legal systems to hold people responsible for their actions and to restore God's order whenever and wherever possible. God does not expect, however, every sin to be declared illegal by human government. Rather, He expects a system of law that maintains both order and liberty by promoting justice as much as humanly possible.

The Bible tells what is good and what God requires of mankind: "to act justly, and to love faithfulness, and to walk humbly with your God" (Micah 6:8). The Christian's motivation to "do justly" is knowing that "The LORD is slow to anger but great in power; the LORD will never leave the guilty unpunished" (Nahum 1:3). His motivation to "love mercy" and "walk humbly" is the supreme example of the Law-giver himself—Jesus Christ—who showed mercy and walked humbly and told the woman taken in adultery, "Neither do I condemn you, . . .Go, and from now on, do not sin any more" (John 8:11). As Christians, we know we cannot live the perfect life exemplified by Christ, but we may also be assured that, because of God's grace, Christ will speak these same words to His followers on the day of judgment.

RECOMMENDED READING FOR ADVANCED STUDY:
LAW

Bastiat, Frederic. *The Law.* Irvington-On-Hudson, New York: The Foundation of Economic Education, 1996.

Bork, Robert H. *The Tempting of America: The Political Seduction of the Law.* New York: The Free Press, 1990.

Budziszewski, J. *Written on the Heart: The Case for Natural Law.* Downers Grove, Ill.: InterVarsity Press, 1997.

House, H. Wayne, ed. *Restoring the Constitution.* Dallas, Tex.: Probe, 1987.

Whitehead, John W. *The Second American Revolution.* Westchester, Ill.: Crossway, 1988.

ENDNOTES

1. Carl F.H. Henry, *Twilight of a Great Civilization* (Westchester, Ill.: Crossway Books, 1988), p. 147.

2. John W. Whitehead, *The Second American Revolution* (Westchester, Ill.: Crossway Books, 1988), p. 80.

3. R. J. Rummel, *Death by Government* (New Brunswick, N.J.: Transaction Publishers, 1994), p. 9.

4. John Warwick Montgomery, *The Law Above the Law* (Minneapolis: Dimension Books, 1975), p. 26.

5. A.E. Wilder-Smith, *The Creation of Life* (Costa Mesa, Ca.: TWFT Publishers, 1970), p.ix.

6. Whitehead, *The Second American Revolution,* p. 21.

7. Ibid., p. 73.

8. William Blackstone, "Commentaries on the Laws of England," in *Blackstone's Commentaries with Notes of Reference to the Constitution and Laws of the Federal Government of the United States and of the Commonwealth of Virginia,* five volumes, ed. St. George Tucker (Philadelphia: William Young Birch and Abraham Small, 1803; reprint, South Hackensack, N.J.: Rothman Reprints, 1969), vol. 1, p. 38-9.

9. Blackstone, p. 58.

10. Whitehead, *The Second American Revolution,* p. 76.

11. Ibid., p. 87-8.

12. Montgomery, *The Law Above the Law,* p. 47.

13. Francis A. Schaeffer, "Joshua and the Flow of Biblical History," *The Complete Works,* Vol. 2, p. 249.

14. Gary T. Amos, *Defending the Declaration* (Brentwood, Tenn.: Wolgemuth and Hyatt, 1989), p. 109.

15. Ibid., p. 117.

16. Rousas John Rushdoony, *The Politics of Guilt and Pity* (Fairfax, Va.: Thoburn Press, 1978), p. 135.

17. John Eidsmoe, *God and Caesar* (Westchester, Ill.: Crossway Books, 1985), p. 197.

18. Simon Greenleaf, *A Treatise on the Law of Evidence* (1824), Part V, Section 29, n. 1, cited in Herbert Titus, *God, Man, and Law: The Biblical Principles* (2d temporary ed., 1983), p. 85.

CHAPTER 9

Politics

KEY QUESTIONS

What is the purpose of government?

KEY IDEA

Human government was instituted by God to protect man's unalienable rights from mankind's sinful tendencies.

KEY QUOTE

"Christianity teaches that the state serves a divinely appointed and divinely defined task, although it is not in itself divine. Its authority is legitimate, though limited."[1]

—CHUCK COLSON

SUMMARY

Biblical Christianity recognizes the state as a God-ordained institution (Genesis 9:6, Romans 13:1-7, 1 Peter 2:13-17). Christianity believes in the depravity of man (Jeremiah 17:9) and his moral responsibility and therefore that government is a necessary institution—even to the imposition of the death penalty (Genesis 9:6, Romans 13:1-4). However, government has God-ordained limits, not totalitarian powers.

The Bible calls for limited government, falling somewhere between no government (anarchy) and total government (totalitarianism). Caesar has his role, but, according to biblical social and legal theory, God has also appointed separate roles for the family and the church.

Throughout history, mankind has accepted the existence of the state, believing it to be "as unavoidable as death and taxes." The Christian believes this certainty arises because government is an institution established by God (Genesis 9:6).Christians recognize that government as an institution is sacred and that its rulers are ministers of God (Romans 13). It is the Christian's duty to obey the state. "Submit to every human institution because of the Lord," says Peter, "whether to the Emperor as the supreme authority, or to governors as those sent out by him to punish those who do evil and to praise those who do good" (1 Peter 2:13-14). Government is appointed by God, so as long as it is serving the purpose for which God created it, the Christian shows allegiance to God by submitting to human government.

> *Genesis 9:6 Whoever sheds man's blood, by man his blood will be shed, for in the image of God He made man.*

> **Government is appointed by God, so as long as it is serving the purpose for which God created it, the Christian shows allegiance to God by submitting to human government.**

The Christian expects the state to accomplish limited, God-ordained tasks. Government should adhere to the principle, "everything must be done decently and in order" (1 Corinthians 14:40; Exodus 18:19f) since this is a reflection of God's character. Further, it should be participatory, so that Christian citizens can better influence the state to conform to God's will as a social institution (Proverbs 11:11). The Christian also understands that power tends to corrupt, so that a government that disperses power is better than one that gathers power into the hands of a few. Christianity, however, does not single out any particular form of government as the only acceptable one. Rather, it expects any type of government to conform to biblical principles, understanding that this is more likely to occur in a representative form of government than in a dictatorship.

> *"Our Constitution was made only for a moral and religious people. It is wholly inadequate for the government of any other."*
> —JOHN ADAMS, PRESIDENT OF THE UNITED STATES, 1797–1801

The aspects of American government that most closely conform to the

Christian ideal are, not surprisingly, the most valuable part of America's political heritage. These include America's division of governmental power into three branches—legislative, executive, and judicial—and the concordant system of checks and balances.

CREATION AND ORIGINAL SIN

Perhaps the Christian concept America's founders best understood was the Christian view of human nature. The United States was born in an environment in which men held a Christian view of mankind's fallen nature, but they did not forget that people also are created in the image of God. These two beliefs have profound implications for a Christian view of politics, which is reflected in America's founding fathers' attempts to tailor a government suited to mankind's place in God's creative order.

Human government became necessary because of the fall. Since every person is inherently sinful, our evil inclinations must be kept in check by laws and by a government capable of enforcing such laws. Thus, government protects mankind from its own sinful nature. But who protects the society from the sinful inclinations of those who make up the government? This was the problem with which America's early leaders grappled in attempting to create a just political system.

They solved the problem by creating a system of checks and balances within the government. America was designed in such a way that each of the three branches of government has unique powers that prevent the focus of governmental authority from falling into the hands of a select few. By broadly distributing

"If men were angels, no government would be necessary."—James Madison, president of the United States, 1809-17

power and responsibility, the American system removes much of the opportunity for man's sinful nature to misuse political clout.

As James Madison says, "If men were angels, no government would be necessary. If angels were to govern men, neither external nor internal controls on government would be necessary." [2] This Christian understanding of humanity helped form a more practical government than that of governments built on a faulty view of human nature.

> *"The rights of man come not from the generosity of the state, but from the hand of God."*
> —JOHN F. KENNEDY, PRESIDENT OF THE UNITED STATES, 1961-[3]

Further, a Christian worldview is indispensable for guaranteeing basic human rights for individuals. Because Christians believe people are created in the image of God, they believe that each individual has value (this becomes doubly clear when we remember that Christ took upon Himself human flesh and died for mankind). Each individual is granted by God certain rights founded on an absolute moral standard. This is the second facet of Christian belief that greatly affects Christian political theory.

> **The Declaration of Independence assumes, first, that man was created by a supernatural Being and second, that this Being is the foundation for all human rights.**

This aspect of the Christian view of man was also taken into account by America's forefathers. Thus, in the Declaration of Independence, we find the proclamation that "all men are created equal; that they are endowed by their Creator with certain unalienable rights." Two assumptions are inherent in this declaration: first, man was created by a supernatural Being; second, this Being is the foundation for all human rights.

The fact that these unalienable rights have an unchanging Source is crucial for Christian politics. If rights were not tied inextricably to the character of God, then human rights would be arbitrarily assigned according to the whims of each passing generation. Rights are "unalienable" only because they are based on God's unchanging character. God established government to secure these rights. This protection of human rights is God's basic purpose for government.

THE PURPOSE OF GOVERNMENT

According to the biblical Christian worldview, human government was instituted by God to protect each person's unalienable rights from mankind's sinful tendencies (Genesis 9:6; Romans 13:1-7). Human nature being what it is, people will attempt to infringe on other's rights in an effort to improve their own lives. Therefore a political system must exist to protect rights and keep these evil tendencies at bay.

Taking into account that people in power have the same sinful nature as everyone else, America's founders built a system of checks and balances into the U.S. Constitution.

Protecting human rights from evil tendencies, of course, simply means promoting justice. And what is justice? E. Calvin Beisner says justice and truth are interrelated, for justice is the practice of truth in human relationships. He concludes that "justice is rendering to each his due according to a right standard."[3]

Most everyone believes that furthering justice is an important task of the state, but the Christian sees justice as the principal reason for the state's existence. Such a view of justice is grounded in an absolute Guarantor of unalienable rights. Because of this, promoting justice becomes more important than any other aspect of government. Rousas Rushdoony is correct to assert that whether a man "can vote or not is not nearly as important as the question of justice: does the law leave him secure in his governmental spheres, as an individual, a family, church, school, or business?"[4]

Government, according to this view, has limited responsibility. The state should concentrate on enforcing justice and avoid meddling in the business of other institutions. It must never assume the responsibilities of other institutions, including church and family. Generally speaking, the church's responsibility is to manifest God's grace on the earth, and the family's responsibility is to manifest God's community and creativity (including procreativity).

Each of these institutions is limited by its own definition as well as by the other two institutions. Because government is an institution of justice, not of grace, community or creativity, it should not interfere with freedom of religion, nor attempt to dispense grace through tax-funded handouts, to control family size, to interfere in raising children (including education), or to control the economy. Government has a role; it should allow other God-ordained institutions the freedom to perform their roles.

The state is responsible to enforce justice, but equally important, it is to avoid interfering with the God-ordained responsibilities of family and church.

SOVEREIGNTY APART FROM GOD

Unfortunately, human government almost always winds up overstepping its God-ordained bounds. Today, many leaders (both in politics and in other disciplines) do not understand mankind's true place in the universe, and this incorrect perspective results in the usurpation of God's sovereignty. Anything that is elevated to a position rightfully belonging only to God is assuming authority that is not rightfully its own to wield (Psalm 103:19).

Abandoning God and placing trust in an individual or in the state will always result in a power-mad and abusive state. Charles Colson explains, "Excise belief in God and you are left with only two principals: the individual and the state. In this situation, however, there is no mediating structure to generate moral values and, therefore, no counterbalance

Psalms 103:19 The Lord has established His throne in heaven, and His kingdom rules over all.

to the inevitable ambitions of the state."[5] "If we are not governed by God," says William Penn, "then we will be ruled by tyrants."[6]

Many today, including both Secular Humanists and Marxist/Leninists, are calling for a world state to serve as the ultimate political and economic authority and to assist mankind on its evolutionary journey. If the Marxists and humanists get their way (and there is plenty of movement toward "a new world order"), it will be not only the Kingdom of Man but also the Kingdom of the Anti-Christ.

> *"If we are not governed by God, then we will be ruled by tyrants."*
> —WILLIAM PENN

UTOPIANISM

Utopianism is a prime example of man's denial of God, placing absolute sovereignty in the hands of the state. This mistake results not only from willing disregard of God's ultimate authority but also from a misconception about human nature. For example, both Marxists and humanists believe in the perfectibility of humankind, and this belief leads them to conclude that once the correct environment is manufactured for all people and their minds are programmed correctly, everyone will live properly. The state (with proper input from the humanists or Marxists, of course) becomes the manufacturer of the correct environment. The state quickly takes on the role of God.

This belief in mankind's perfectibility (called by Colson "the most subtle and dangerous delusion of our times"[7]) is seen in our present society's denial of individual responsibility. Denying individual responsibility separates people from their only possible salvation—a knowledge and acceptance of Christ's sacrifice for the individual's sins—and condemns secular people to an endless search for the "proper utopian environment."

Karl Marx co-authored the *Communist Manifesto* with his close friend and financial supporter, Frederick Engels, in 1848.

Joseph Stalin *(1879–1953)*

1899 Expelled from the Tpilsi theological seminary
1902 Arrested for revolutionary Marxist activities and banished to Siberia
1904 Helps fund the Bolsheviks by organizing bank robberies
1922 Appointed secretary general of the Secretariat of the USSR
1927 Gains control of USSR
1927 Begins systematic "liquidation" of Ukranians, killing more than 10 million people
1935 Signs pact with Adolf Hilter that aligns the USSR with Nazi Germany
1945 Creates Yalta agreement with Franklin D. Roosevelt and Winston Churchill

---

Indeed, utopianism offers no salvation except through the hope that the state will someday create the perfect environment and perfect human beings. Colson says, "While Christian teaching emphasizes that each person has worth and responsibility before God, utopianism argues that salvation can only be achieved collectively."[8] This reliance on the state results in the individual being trampled underfoot. History provides many chilling examples of this—most notably, Joseph Stalin's slaughter of millions of innocent "bourgeois."

The lack of legitimate authority that results from the denial of God reinforces the Christian's belief that God must be recognized as Ruler in every sphere, including politics. Infringements on human rights by various governments based on the sovereignty or whim of the state speaks eloquently of the need for a transcendent law.

A QUESTION OF OBEDIENCE

The Christian expects a lot from government. The state must recognize man's place in the universe and understand God as the ultimate source of authority and human rights. Conversely, God expects the Christian to respect, obey, and participate in governments that serve His will (Romans 13:1-2).

The reason God demands this is simple: government exists to promote justice. Obedience to just government is necessary to keep the need for governmental power at a minimum. Thus, the Christian is called to obey the government, to honor justice, and to preserve order. However, this does not mean that Christians must obey government blindly. The political leader has a responsibility to God, and the Christian must hold him accountable.

When a political leader or government strays from obedience, the Christian must attempt to correct the deviance so that he or she will not be forced to disobey the state. This may involve registering to vote and voting; it may involve passing out petitions. Some Christians will be called to run for political office, and others will be called to serve in nonelected offices. Such involvement is a more effective way than civil disobedience to peacefully persuade government to be obedient to God. If the people rejoice when the righteous rule (Proverbs 29:2), the righteous need to rule.

Proverbs 29:2 When the righteous flourish, the people rejoice, but when the wicked rule, people groan.

But what if a Christian becomes as politically involved as possible and still is faced with certain governmental policies that are unjust and therefore displeasing to God? As noted earlier, the Bible clearly instructs people to obey God even when His commands conflict with those in authority. Acts 4:19 says that when the Sanhedrin commanded Peter and John to stop teaching about Jesus, they replied, "Whether it's right in the sight of God for us to listen to you rather than to God, you decide."

Daniel 6:10 When Daniel learned that the document had been signed, he went into his house. The windows in its upper room opened toward Jerusalem, and three times a day he got down on his knees, prayed, and gave thanks to his God, just as he had done before.

This obedience to God is required even after the Christian has worked for reform through all possible political channels. If the system remains unjust, it becomes necessary for the Christian to engage in acts of civil disobedience in order to remain obedient to God. Francis Schaeffer sums up: "The bottom line is that at a certain point there is not only the right, but the duty, to disobey the state."[9] This disobedience may even result in being put to death by the state. In such instances it is better to die than to live. Daniel understood this truth and chose death over worshiping a king (Daniel 6:1-10). God honors such commitment.

CONCLUSION

God established the state to administer justice. When government rules within the proper boundaries of its role in God's plan, the Christian submits to the state because God has placed it in authority over him. However, when the state abuses that authority, or claims to be sovereign, the Christian acknowledges the transcendent law of God rather than the state. This loyalty to God motivates the Christian to become politically involved in an effort to create good and just government. The involvement of righteous people can significantly influence government for the better.

This constant battle by the Christian to create or maintain a just state may or may not have an effect on government policy. That's not the important issue. What is important is that the Christian remains obedient to God under all circumstances. Colson writes, "Christians are to do their duty as best they can. But even when they feel that they are making no difference, that they are failing to bring Christian values to the public arena, success is not the criteria. Faithfulness is." [10]

RECOMMENDED READING FOR ADVANCED STUDY: POLITICS

Amos, Gary, and Richard Gardiner. *Never Before in History: America's Inspired Birth*. Dallas: Haughton, 1998.

Barton, David. *Original Intent: The Courts, the Constitution, and Religion*. Aledo, Tex.: WallBuilders Press, 1997.

Evans, M. Stanton. *The Theme Is Freedom: Religion, Politics, and the American Tradition*. Washington, D.C.: Regnery, 1994.

Federer, William J. *America's God and Country Encyclopedia of Quotations*. Coppell, Tex.: Fame, 1996.

Schaeffer, Francis A. *A Christian Manifesto*. Wheaton, Ill.: Crossway Books, 1982.

ENDNOTES

1. Charles Colson, *Kingdoms in Conflict* (Grand Rapids, Mich.: Zondervan, 1987), p. 92.

2. James Madison, *The Federalist Papers,* no. 51 (New York: Pocket Books, 1964), p. 122.

3. E. Calvin Beisner, *Prosperity and Poverty: The Compassionate Use of Resources in a World of Scarcity* (Westchester, Ill.: Crossway Books, 1988) p. 45.

4. Rousas John Rushdoony, *Politics of Guilt and Pity* (Fairfax, Va.: Thoburn Press, 1978), p. 239.

5. Colson, *Kingdoms in Conflict,* p. 226.

6. Francis A. Schaeffer, *A Christian Manifesto* (Westchester, Ill.: Crossway Books, 1982), p. 34.

7. Charles Colson, *Who Speaks for God?* (Westchester, Ill.: Crossway Books, 1988) p. 144.

8. Colson, *Kingdoms in Conflict,* p. 77.

9. Schaeffer, *A Christian Manifesto,* p. 93. An example of the proper time for disobedience recently arose when the American government (through its public health services) advised churches to amend their attitude toward homosexuality. The Bible clearly dictates the proper Christian response to homosexuality (see Romans 1 and Jude 1), and the church must stand firm in her commitment to obey God's dictums even when they conflict with those of the state.

10. Colson, *Kingdoms in Conflict,* p. 291.

CHAPTER 10

Economics

KEY QUESTION

What produces a sound economy?

KEY IDEA

In God's wonderful plan, the duty to work gives rise to the right to property, which in turn creates the duty to use the property wisely.

KEY QUOTES

"The commandment 'Thou shalt not steal' is the clearest declaration of the right to private property in the Old Testament."

—IRVING E. HOWARD

SUMMARY

Christians begin their economic theory with an assumption about human nature. The Bible declares that man is sinful. Another biblical precept—the concept of justice—also plays an important role for the Christian. The most desirable economic system promotes justice by protecting the rights of individuals from infringement by others. If all people were inherently good, one might not have to worry about individuals denying the rights of others, but people are not inherently good. Therefore, Christians believe the best economic system assures checks and balances that guarantee the protection of human rights.

Applying this criterion, Christians believe the free enterprise system to be more compatible with their worldview than any other economic system. Economic systems that check injustice and grant responsibility to people—in terms both of private property and of economic decisions—allow the freedom for all to act with the dignity of beings created in God's image. This, according to the Christian view, is the important end of economic theory: offering people not riches or luxury, but the freedom to seek fulfillment through pursuing their role in God's universe.

Christians are divided on the issue of economics. While many believe the Bible teaches an economic system of private property and individual responsibilities and initiatives (citing Isaiah 65:21-2; Jeremiah 32:43-4; Acts 5:1-4; Ephesians 4:28), many others are adamant in their support of a socialist or public property economy (citing Acts 2:44-45). In fact, some Christians proclaim that the Bible teaches a form of economic Marxism. These people—"liberation theologians"—expect some form of socialism to usher in the kingdom of heaven.

Although no economic system can save mankind, capitalism is the system most compatible with the teachings of Scripture.

Such thinking is a trap of which every Christian must beware, because no economic system—whether communist, socialist, capitalist, or any combination—is capable of saving mankind. No economic system is perfect. This does not mean, however, that all economic systems are equal. One system, in fact, is quite compatible with God's Word and our profoundly imperfect world.

SOCIALISM OR FREE ENTERPRISE?

At the most basic level, the Christian is faced with supporting either socialism or free enterprise. In the real world, neither socialism nor capitalism exists in "pure" form. That is, all capitalist systems contain certain elements of socialism, and vice versa. But for our purposes, we will discuss these opposing systems in terms of their least diluted manifestations.

> *"Men must choose between capitalism and socialism."*
> —LUDWIG VON MISES

The simplest distinction between socialism and the free market system is outlined by Ronald Nash: "One dominant feature of capitalism is economic freedom, the right of people to exchange things voluntarily, free from force, fraud, and theft. Capitalism is more than this, of course, but its concern with free [and peaceful] exchange [of goods and services] is obvious. Socialism, on the other hand, seeks to replace the freedom of the market with a group of central planners who exercise control over essential market functions."[1] Christians who believe socialism (or communism) is the more desirable system trust that this centralized control will create a more just means of distributing scarce resources. They believe the Bible supports their call for socialism, often pointing to Acts 2:44-5 as evidence that God's Word calls for such an economic arrangement. Acts 2:44-5, however, must be seen in the context of Acts 2:5 which describes the church's unique situation at the time. When one studies the Bible as a whole, it becomes obvious that God's Word is much more supportive of an economic system respecting private property, the work ethic, and personal responsibility (see especially Isaiah 65:21-2; Jeremiah 32:43-4; Proverbs 31; Acts 5:1-4; Ephesians 4:28).

> When one studies the Bible as a whole, it becomes obvious that God's Word is much more supportive of an economic system respecting private property, the work ethic, and personal responsibility.

> *Acts 2:44-5 Now all the believers were together and had everything in common. 45 So they sold their possessions and property and distributed the proceeds to all, as anyone had a need.*

PRIVATE PROPERTY

Christians who adhere to socialism claim that private property encourages greed and envy and that public ownership removes such temptation to sin. But is this compatible with Scripture? Irving E. Howard doesn't think so: "The commandment 'Thou shalt not steal' is the clearest declaration of the right to private property in the Old Testament."[2] In fact, private ownership and stewardship of prop-

> *Acts 2:5 There were Jews living in Jerusalem, devout men from every nation under heaven.*

erty is assumed to be the proper state of affairs throughout the Bible (Deuteronomy 8; Ruth 2; Isaiah 65:21-2; Jeremiah 32:42-44; Micah 4:1-4; Luke 12:13-15; Acts 5:1-4; Ephesians 4:28). E. Calvin Beisner demonstrates this by asking, "Why does Scripture require restitution, including multiple restitution, in cases of theft, even if paying the restitution requires selling oneself into slavery (Exodus 22:1ff)?"[3] Clearly, Scripture requires this because God has bestowed on mankind a right to property.

This right to property stems from our duty to work. After casting Adam and Eve out of Eden, God decreed that mankind must face a life of toil (Genesis 3:17-19). But God, in His mercy, allowed that people who conscientiously adhere to this duty may be rewarded with private property. Proverbs 10:4 states, "Whoever works with a lazy hand becomes poor, but a diligent hand brings riches." God has designed a world in which the existence of private property encourages people to be responsible and fruitful.

Further, since God grants people private ownership as stewards of His creation, they become accountable to God for the way in which they use property. In God's wonderfully intricate plan, the duty to work gives rise to the right to property, which in turn creates the duty to use the property wisely. Beisner states, "Biblical stewardship views God as Owner of all things (Psalm 24:1) and man—

The right to own property stems from our duty to work and encourages people to be responsible and fruitful.

individually and collectively—as His steward. Every person is accountable to God for the use of whatever he has (Genesis 1:26-30; 2:15). Every person's responsibility as a steward is to maximize the Owner's return on His investment by using it to serve others (Matthew 25:14-30)."[4]

This use of property to serve others can only occur in a society in which property is privately owned. Publicly owned property destroys a person's sense of responsibility to use possessions wisely, because there is no incentive for selfish or lazy people to treat the property wisely. Let's admit a simple economic truism: men and women who own property take better care of it than those who don't own property.

Private property, from the Christian perspective, actually discourages greed and envy by causing people to focus on the need to work and serve others rather than accumulate more for themselves. When one understands property in the context of stewardship, it becomes obvious that private property encourages a more careful attitude toward scarce resources than does public property.

> Private property encourages a more careful attitude toward scarce resources than does public property.

At this point, however, the socialist may argue that we live in an imperfect world and that one cannot expect everyone always to have an attitude of stewardship. This, unfortunately, is true. But is the socialist's conclusion—that allowing selfish people to compete in a free market system for limited property leads to counterproductive actions—necessarily true? Is economic competition inherently evil?

ECONOMIC COMPETITION

Judging from verses noted such as Proverbs 10:4, 14:23, and Luke 10:7, it would seem that the Bible calls for men to compete with each other in the workplace to encourage fruitfulness. When this biblical principle is applied, it turns out to be very practical. Economic competition tends to stifle man's sinful tendencies. The reason for this is quite obvious: an individual in business must be on his or her best behavior or customers will go to the competition. The entrepreneur must also look out for the customers' best interests, or they also can go to the competition.

> Economic competition tends to stifle man's sinful tendencies.

Competition encourages cooperation in a capitalist society, because the people involved act in accordance with the principle of comparative advantage. This principle states that every member of a free market society can produce a valuable good or service by specializing in an area in which he or she is at the least disadvantage, thus producing something of value to others. Individuals find that they can be more successful in a free market by focusing their energies on production that is beneficial to society as a whole—that is, by cooperating. This, in turn, creates additional goods and services which become more readily available to poorer members of society.

When viewed from the perspective of comparative advantage, competition also creates another benefit: it promotes the worth of each individual. The free market preserves each person's dignity by granting the individual the opportunity to contribute to the welfare of the society.

A person in business must look out for his customers' best interests, or they can go to the competition.

Comparative advantage allows everyone to be the "best" producer of some service or product. This meshes perfectly with the biblical perspective, which describes each individual as intrinsically valuable because all are made in the image of God.

Competition, when it leads to cooperation and recognition of individual worth, fits the Christian worldview. Indeed, when one understands that the only alternative to competition is contrary to biblical revelation, one must admit the value of a capitalist or free and peaceful system.

Or so it seems. However, Christians who view socialism as the proper economic system have an ace in the hole. They claim that "social" justice demands that each individual possess an equal share of scarce resources and that this primary principle overrules all other considerations.

THE PRINCIPLE OF "SOCIAL" JUSTICE

On the surface, demanding economic equality seems quite noble. What could be fairer than every man sharing equally in the scarce resources available? But we have already demonstrated that God's Word calls for private property, and further, we are faced with the disturbing words of the Apostle Paul in 2 Thessalonians 3:10: "In fact, when we were with you, this is what we commanded you: 'If anyone isn't willing to work, he should not eat.'" How does one reconcile the seemingly noble notion of economic equality with such straightforward biblical truth?

The answer, of course, is that one cannot. Beisner quotes Leviticus 19:15 and concludes, "God is not 'on the side of the poor,' despite protests to the contrary. Any law, therefore, that gives an advantage in the economic sphere to anyone, rich or poor, violates Biblical justice."[5] Why is this the case? Because justice requires equality before the law, not equality of incomes or abilities.

> 2 Thessalonians 3:10 In fact, when we were with you, this is what we commanded you: 'If anyone isn't willing to work, he should not eat.'

Indeed, justice will necessarily lead to economic inequality. As Beisner says, "the Bible demands impartiality, which—because people differ in interests, gifts, capacities, and stations in life—must invariably result in conditional inequality."[6]

Justice is based not on equal income but on opportunity equally unhindered by coercive shackles. "Given the diversity and liberty of human life," says Michael Novak, "no fair and free system

> **Justice requires equality before the law, not equality of incomes or abilities.**

can possibly guarantee equal outcomes. A democratic system depends for its legitimacy, therefore, not upon equal results but upon a sense of equal opportunity."[7] And equal opportunity means not that everyone must start with the same skills and social contacts, but that no one must be prohibited by law from attempting something morally legitimate in the marketplace.

THE RICH AND THE POOR

Much of the reason the Christian socialist insists upon the need for economic equality lies in the mistaken assumption that the rich extract their wealth from the poor. If this view were correct, the socialist call for economic equality might be justified. However, this view is out of touch with reality. First, the Bible makes it clear that poverty does not always result from exploitation by the rich.

Nash says

> **It is certainly true, that Scripture recognizes that poverty sometimes results from oppression and exploitation. But Scripture also teaches that there are times when poverty results from misfortunes that have nothing to do with exploitation. These misfortunes include such things as accidents, injuries, and illness. And of course the Bible also makes it plain that poverty can result from indigence and sloth (Proverbs 6:6-11; 13:4; 24:30-34; 28:19).[8]**

Second, in free market economies, the wealthy ordinarily create more wealth. Socialists would have us view rich individuals as hoarding already scarce resources—but in truth, the wealthy use the free market effectively to multiply the goods and services available. This, in turn, creates more opportunity for rich and poor alike. "Under capitalism," explains George Gilder, "when it is working, the rich have the anti-Midas touch . . . turning gold into goods and jobs and art."[9]

In this way, the rich aid the poor by constantly expanding the pool of wealth and opportunity. Gilder also explains that "most real wealth originates in individual minds in unpredictable and uncontrollable ways. A successful economy depends on the proliferation of the rich, on creating a large class of risk-taking men who are willing to shun the easy channels of a comfortable life in order to create new enterprise, win huge profits, and invest them again."[10] The free market encourages the wealthy to invest their wealth in productive enterprises, thus making jobs, goods, and services available to others. But a socialist economy encourages the wealthy to hide their wealth from taxation by hoarding it in the form of foreign bank accounts, superfluous luxuries, and other nonproductive uses. This is a fundamental truth that socialists ignore: wealth comes more from the mental creativity and physical hard work fostered by free enterprise than from the resources themselves. Indeed, resources are not strictly natural at all; they are all made by the application of human thought and energy to the raw materials around us. Land in and of itself produces only weeds and an occasional berry; land under the guidance of a farmer's creativity and hard work yields fruit and vegetables for an entire community.

> In free market economies, the wealthy ordinarily create more wealth.

Wealth is generated through the creativity and hard work fostered by free enterprise.

FREEDOM AND ECONOMICS

We began our analysis of capitalism and socialism by noting that capitalism trusts the free market while socialism requires centralized control. From this most fundamental difference between the two systems springs a number of ramifications, including the counterproductive bureaucracies created by the welfare system in the United States. Because socialism requires a planned economy, including control over wealth distribution, pricing, and production, it also requires a powerful central government to initiate the plans. As P. T. Bauer points out, "Attempts to minimize economic differences in an open and free society necessarily involve the use of coercive power."[11] Thus, the socialist must rely upon increased political power to achieve the goals of economic equality and a planned economy.

In a capitalist system, by contrast, far less political power is necessary, because the government need not worry about controlling incomes, prices, or production. Citizens are free to determine how they will spend their money and how they will use their resources.

Clearly, there is a relationship between the type of economy a society chooses and the amount of freedom the individual must sacrifice. In a socialist society, the individual must relinquish to the government much of the control over his life. "The only way to arrive at equal fruits is to equalize behavior," says Beisner, "and that requires robbing men of liberty, making them slaves."[12] Economic freedom and the right to private property are crucial for political freedom.

> In a capitalist system, . . . citizens are free to determine how they will spend their money and how they will use their resources.

CONCLUSION

The Christian worldview embraces democratic capitalism or the free and peaceful exchange of goods and services for a number of reasons. The Bible not only grants mankind the right to private property but also calls for people to be good stewards of their property—and the free enterprise system affords the greatest chance to act as responsible stewards by creating wealth and opportunity. Further, the competition in a free market works according to the principle of comparative advantage, which affirms the inherent worth of every individual.

> Economic freedom and the right to private property are crucial for political freedom.

Capitalism is also more just than socialism. While the socialist calls for economic equality, capitalism respects the biblical requirement of equality before the law. This does not, as the socialist contends, cause the rich to get richer and the poor poorer. Rather, it encourages the rich to create more wealth, thereby aiding all of society. The policies of redistribution, including welfare systems, only multiply the problems of the poor—creating needless bureaucracies and concentrating too much power in the hands of government bureaucrats. Conversely, capitalism encourages freedom in the political sphere. This removes the danger of granting excessive sovereignty to the state instead of to God.

The Christian who accepts the Bible must also accept democratic capitalism or free enterprise as the system most compatible with the biblical worldview. This truth was apparent even to the champion of Communism, Frederick Engels: "[I]f some few passages of the Bible may be favourable to Communism, the general spirit of its doctrines is, nevertheless, totally opposed to it." [13]

RECOMMENDED READING FOR ADVANCED STUDY: ECONOMICS

Bauer, P. T. *Equality, the Third World, and Economic Delusion.* Cambridge, Mass.: Harvard University Press, 1981.

Beisner, E. Calvin. *Prosperity and Poverty: The Compassionate Use of Resources in a World of Scarcity.* Wheaton, Ill.: Crossway Books, 1988.

Bethell, Tom. *The Noblest Triumph: Property and Prosperity Through the Ages.* New York: St. Martin's Press, 1998.

Gilder, George. *Wealth and Poverty.* New York: Basic Books, 1981.

Nash, Ronald H. *Poverty and Wealth: The Christian Debate Over Capitalism.* Westchester, Ill.: Crossway, 1987.

ENDNOTES

1. Ronald Nash, *Poverty and Wealth: The Christian Debate Over Capitalism* (Westchester, Ill.: Crossway Books, 1987), p. 63.

2. Irving E. Howard, *The Christian Alternative to Socialism* (Arlington, Va.: Better Books, 1966), p. 43.

3. E. Calvin Beisner, *Prosperity and Poverty: The Compassionate Use of Resources in a World of Scarcity* (Westchester, Ill.: Crossway Books, 1988), p. 66.

4. Ibid., p. xi-xii.

5. Ibid., p. 52.

6. Ibid.

7. Novak, *The Spirit of Democratic Capitalism*, p. 15.

8. Nash, *Poverty and Wealth*, p. 71.

9. George Gilder, *Wealth and Poverty* (New York: Basic Books, 1981), p. 63.

10. Ibid, p. 245. For further discussion of the role of mind in economics, see Warren Brookes' excellent work, *The Economy in Mind* (New York: Universe Books, 1982).

11. P.T. Bauer, *Equality, the Third World, and Economic Delusion* (Cambridge, Mass.: Harvard University Press, 1981), p. 18.

12. Beisner, *Prosperity and Poverty*, p. 54.

13. Karl Marx and Frederick Engels, *Collected Works,* forty volumes (New York: International Publishers, 1976), vol. 3, p. 399.

CHAPTER 11

History

KEY QUESTION

How should we interpret human events?

KEY IDEA

Archaeology has consistently supported the assertion that the Bible is a trustworthy historical document.

KEY QUOTE

"The importance of the Biblical conception [of history] cannot be overstressed. Here for the first time Western man was presented with a purposive, goal-directed interpretation of history."

—JOHN WARWICK MONTGOMERY

SUMMARY

Christianity and history have always been allies. The Bible is rooted in the story of God's involvement with mankind, and without the historical resurrection of Jesus Christ there would be no Christian worldview (1 Corinthians 15:14-5). The history recounted by the Bible is accurate, and the events described in it actually occurred.

The historical Bible (the written Word) and Jesus Christ (the living Word) are the two cornerstones of the Christian worldview. If the Bible is not history, or if Jesus Christ is not "God with us" (Matthew 1:23), the Savior of mankind (2 Timothy 1:10), biblical Christianity crumbles. Biblical history begins and ends with Jesus Christ, the "Alpha and Omega" (Revelation 22:13).

Christians believe the basis for their worldview appeared in human history in the form of Jesus Christ about two thousand years ago. While "Christ died for our sins" is orthodox Christian theology, "Christ died" is history. To shatter Christian doctrine and the Christian worldview, one would need only to shatter its historical underpinnings.

> Christians believe the basis for their worldview appeared in human history in the form of Jesus Christ about two thousand years ago.

The Christian also believes that the Bible is God's revealed Word in the form of a trustworthy book grounded in history. Thus, for the Christian, history is supremely important. Either Christ is a historical figure, and the Bible is a historical document that describes God's communications with humankind and records events in the life of Christ, or the Christian faith is bankrupt (1 Corinthians 15:14).

> The Christian also believes that the Bible is God's revealed Word in the form of a trustworthy book grounded in history.

History is as important for the Christian worldview as it is for the Marxist/Leninist and the Secular Humanist worldviews. And if the Christian perspective is correct, history has already revealed the worldview that fits the facts of reality. While the humanist (both Secular and Cosmic) and the Marxist see mankind's salvation in the distant future in the form of a utopian society, the Christian sees redemption offered to mankind two thousand years

> 1 Corinthians 15:14 And if Christ has not been raised, then our preaching is without foundation, and so is your faith.

ago and working as powerfully today as it did then. If this is true, then the wise will discover all they can about Jesus Christ.

THE BIBLE AND HISTORY

When considering the claims of Christianity, one question must be asked immediately: Can we trust the Bible to tell us the truth about God's actions in history?

The first area we must explore when judging the historicity of the Bible is the question of authorship. Was the Bible written by eyewitnesses of historical events, or were some books written many years after the fact by men who had only heard vague accounts of the events they attempted to describe? For example, did one of Christ's apostles write the book of Matthew, or did some unknown scribe who had not known Christ write the book in an effort to strengthen the case for Christianity?

Today's scholars have little doubt that the books of the Bible were written largely by eyewitnesses. William F. Albright, a leading twentieth-century archae-ologist, writes, "In my opinion, every book of the New Testament was written by a baptized Jew between the forties and the eighties of the first century (very probably sometime between about A.D. 50 and 75)."[1] Even H.G. Wells, a confirmed atheist, acknowledged that "the four gospels . . . were certainly in existence a few decades after [Christ's] death."[2] The evidence points to the conclusion that the history in the Bible was written by men living in that historical period.

> "In my opinion, every book of the New Testament was written by a baptized Jew between the forties and the eighties of the first century."
>
> —WILLIAM F. ALBRIGHT

However, a second objection arises. Perhaps, say the critics, the Bible was an accurate historical document as it was originally written—but it has been copied and re-copied for thousands of years, and so it has been warped by the inevitable mistakes of copyists. At first glance, this objection seems plausible. But one archaeological discovery made nearly half a century ago destroyed this theory. Gleason L. Archer, Jr. explains: "Even though the two copies of Isaiah discovered in Qumran Cave 1 near the Dead Sea in 1947 were a thousand years earlier than the oldest dated manuscript previously known (A.D. 980), they proved to be word for word identical with our standard Hebrew Bible in more than 95 percent of the text. The 5 percent of variation consisted chiefly of obvious slips of the pen and variations in spelling."[3] That is, a manuscript one thousand years older than the oldest copy of the Bible previously known to exist proved the transmission over that time span to be virtually error-free.

In fact, archaeology has consistently supported the assertion that the Bible is a trustworthy historical document. "It may be stated categorically," says Nelson Glueck, "that no archaeological discovery has ever controverted a biblical reference."[4]

Harvard's Simon Greenleaf (the greatest nineteenth-century authority on the law of evidence in the common law) believed "that the competence of the New Testament documents would be established in any court of law."[5]

One may conclude with confidence that the Bible is an accurate historical document, that the events described in the Old and New Testaments did happen. But this poses a prob-

Archaeology has consistently supported the assertion that the Bible is a trustworthy historical document.

lem for every non-Christian because the Bible states that God became man in Jesus Christ, and if this is true, no other worldview fits the facts of history. Some non-Christians at this point choose a rather illogical means of avoiding the seemingly unavoidable claims of the Bible, suggesting that while the Bible may be true, it does not accurately describe the man known as Jesus Christ. Indeed, some non-Christians go so far as to claim that Jesus Christ never existed. Therefore, we must turn our attention to this aspect of history.

THE HISTORICITY OF CHRIST

The obvious problem faced by people who deny that the Bible accurately describes the life of Jesus Christ is that archaeology and modern criticism have revealed the Bible to be historically accurate. The atheist has no grounds for claiming that man cannot know what Christ did on earth, because the New Testament provides a historical account of His life. However, for the moment we will ignore this key point and touch upon two pieces of outside evidence that confirm the historicity of Christ.

Christ was treated as a historical figure by early historians other than Christians. Around A.D. 93,

> *"Today no competent scholar denies the historicity of Jesus."*
> —BRUCE METZGER

The writings of ancient historians Josephus (A.D. 93) and Cornelius Tacitus (A.D. 112) provide evidence outside of the Bible for the life of Christ.

the Jewish historian Josephus referred to Jesus at least twice in his Antiquities of the Jews. In one instance, he recorded that the high priest Annas "assembled the sanhedrim of the judges, and brought before them the brother of Jesus, who was called Christ, whose name was James . . ." (Antiquities XX.ix.1).

Another early historian, Cornelius Tacitus, wrote around A.D. 112 about "the persons commonly called Christians," and also stated, "Christus, the founder of the name, was put to death by Pontius Pilate, procurator of Judea in the reign of Tiberius: but the pernicious superstition, repressed for a time broke out again, not only through Judea, where the mischief originated, but through the city of Rome also." [6]

These references and others provide sufficient evidence for the historicity of Christ, even when the New Testament is ignored. Bruce Metzger writes:

> **The early non-Christian testimonies concerning Jesus, though scanty, are sufficient to prove (even without taking into account the evidence contained in the New Testament) that he was a historical figure who lived in Palestine in the early years of the first century, that he gathered a group of followers about himself, and that he was condemned to death under Pontius Pilate. Today no competent scholar denies the historicity of Jesus.**[7]

THE RESURRECTION AND HISTORY

The Bible goes out of its way to place its message and major figures in history (see Luke 3:1-2). This is especially true with regard to Christ's resurrection. Luke mentions Pilate, Caesar, Herod, Barabbas, "Joseph, a member of the Sanhedrin," "Arimathaea, a Judean town," and then describes Christ's resurrection as a real event in history (Luke 24:1-7).

The resurrected Christ was witnessed by more than 500 people (1 Corinthians 15:6), including Mary, Peter, and ten other apostles. These witnesses were so moved by the resurrection that they committed their lives to it and to the One whose divinity and righteousness it vindicated. The disciples did not abandon Christ, but instead were willing to die for the truth they were propagating. Indeed, the resurrection of Christ took "a group of scared (Mark 16:8; John 20:19) and skeptical (Luke 24:38; John

> *1 Corinthians 15:6 Then He [Christ] appeared to over five hundred brothers at one time, most of whom remain to the present, but some have fallen asleep.*

> *"The Resurrection is a matter of history open to any who wish to examine the evidence."*
> —NORMAN GEISLER

20:25) men" and transformed them "into courageous evangels who proclaimed the Resurrection in the face of threats on their lives (Acts 4:21; 5:18)!" If the disciples did not consider the resurrection a historical event, is it really conceivable that they would have been willing to die for this kind of testimony?

The faith of modern-day Christians should be no less secure than that of the

> **The faith of modern-day Christians should be no less secure than that of the apostles because it is grounded in historical fact.**

apostles, because it is grounded in historical fact. This fact forms the basis for the biblical Christian worldview and the Christian philosophy of history.

Through the resurrection, God reveals His plan for mankind by conquering sin and guaranteeing a triumphant end to human history. D.W. Bebbington says that since the battle against evil was won by Jesus on the cross, "The outcome of world history is therefore already assured. God will continue to direct the course of events up to

Discovered in a remote cave near the northwest shore of the Dead Sea, the "Dead Sea Scrolls" again confirmed the historical accuracy of the Bible.

their end when the outcome will be made plain."[8] The Christian learns from history that Christ offered Himself up as a perfect sacrifice for mankind, and this is the most important revelation. But the Christian also discovers another important truth: God is active throughout history and plans to lead it to a triumphant conclusion.

While the course of history may seem tragic to some people, the Christian understands that all history is working together for good. Because God became man and died for mankind's sins, the final chapter of history will proclaim the conquering of sin. Thus, Christians are prepared to face difficult, sometimes pain-filled lives, because they understand that the sin that causes pain has been erased from the future. Christians hold no unreasonable expectations for this earthly lifetime—in fact, they anticipate persecution and trials—but do expect to be triumphant in the end because God has come into history to save people from their sinful inclinations.

From the Christian perspective, history is a beautiful unfolding of God's ultimate plan for mankind. Does this mean, however, that only the future holds any value for the Christian? Does the Christian worldview destroy the role of the present in history? The answer is a resounding "no." In the Christian view, God is active throughout history. Therefore, this perspective creates more meaning for every moment of time than does any other worldview. "It is always a 'Now,'" writes Herbert Butterfield, "that is in direct relation to eternity—not a far future; always immediate experience of life that matters in the last resort—not historical constructions based on abridged textbooks or imagined visions of some posterity that is going to be the heir of all the ages."[9]

The central difference between the Christian view of history and that of Marxism and humanism comes down to this one point. Either human history was ordained by God and is directed by Him toward an ultimate conclusion, or human history began due to a random spark in a prebiotic soup and has only chance to thank for its present course.

PURPOSE IN HISTORY

This belief about God's actions in history has vast ramifications for mankind. If the Christian philosophy of history is correct, then not only is the overall story of mankind invested with meaning, but every moment that a person lives is charged with purpose. "Where a God who is totally purposive and totally foreseeing acts upon a Nature which is totally interlocked," explains C.S. Lewis, "there can be no accidents or loose ends, nothing whatever of which we can safely use the word merely. Nothing is 'merely a by-product' of anything else. All results are intended from the first."[10]

Indeed, it is through understanding how God works in our individual lives that we can truly understand how God directs the course of history. Butterfield explains: "[T]here are some people who bring their sins home to themselves and say that this is a chastisement from God; or they say that God is testing them, trying them in the fire, fitting them for some more important work that he has for them to do. Those who adopt this view in their individual lives will easily see that it enlarges and projects itself onto the scale of all history . . ."[11] Purpose and meaning saturate both individual lives and the life of all humanity.

In order to speak accurately about purpose, however, the Christian must speak not only of God's activity throughout history but also of the ultimate goal toward which He is leading mankind. Purpose implies constant supervision by God, a direction for the course of human events, and an ultimate end or goal. For the Christian, history is moving toward a specific climax: the day of judgment (Acts 17:31; Romans 2:11-16). At this point, Christ's victory over sin will become apparent to everyone, and Christians from all of history will be allowed to share in His triumph. This is the good news of Christianity, the truth that makes earthly trials bearable. Paul sums up this faith in Romans 8:18, when he says, "For I consider that the

> *"History after all is the true poetry."*
> —THOMAS CARLYLE

> Purpose and meaning saturate both individual lives and the life of all humanity.

sufferings of this present time are not worth comparing with the glory that is going to be revealed to us."

Ultimately, history is moving toward a triumphant close. Even at this very moment, God is moving human history closer to that end—which, in a real sense, is only the beginning.

THE LINEAR CONCEPTION OF HISTORY

This Christian belief about the direction of history is known as a linear conception of history. That is, human history had a specific beginning (creation), is being directed by God toward a specific end (judgment), and that historic events follow a non-repetitive course toward that end. To the individual living in the Western Hemisphere, this may not seem to be a unique view of history. Doesn't everyone believe that human history had a beginning and moves along a linear path to its end? Most of Western society has a linear view of history—but this view is founded on the Judeo-Christian perspective. Prior to this Christian description of history, Classical thought supported a cyclical view, in which historical events were repeated over and over by consecutive societies. Thus, the Christian view of history did create a unique understanding of the movement of mankind through time. "The importance of the Biblical conception cannot be overstressed," says John Warwick Montgomery. "Here for the first time Western man was presented with a purposive, goal-directed interpretation of history.

All of history is moving toward a triumphant close in the return of Christ.

Direction, as always, comes from God.

The Classical doctrine of recurrence had been able to give a 'substantiality' to history, but it had not given it any aim or direction."[12] Direction, as always, comes from God.

CONCLUSION

Christian history centers on the reliability of the Bible. While we have focused on the most significant event in the biblical Christian worldview (the resurrection of Jesus Christ), the history of the rest of the Bible is also open to close inspection. The Bible's history, as recorded in both Testaments, has stood the test of time.

Secular Humanism, Marxism/Leninism, and Cosmic Humanism all declare that man can save himself, but Christians better understand human nature, and it is this perspective that allows them to form a consistent view regarding the past, the present, and the future. It also helps them understand humankind's role in history. People may freely choose to obey or disobey God, but it is only when they act in obedience that they can affect history positively. Regardless of how this effect happens, God will direct history toward His ultimate end: the day of judgment. This belief in a climactic conclusion causes the Christian to adopt a linear conception of history. This conception reflects the vast meaning with which God has endowed history.

If this historical perspective is correct, then the Christian worldview is proved to be true, and it follows that knowing, accepting, and following Jesus Christ as Savior and Lord is the most important thing anyone can do. Wise men still seek Him, and for good reason. He gives meaning to history, and to life.

RECOMMENDED READING FOR ADVANCED STUDY: HISTORY

Habermas, Gary and Antony Flew. *Did Jesus Rise From the Dead?* New York: Harper and Row, 1987.

Kennedy, D. James and Jerry Newcombe. *What if the Bible Had Never Been Written?* Nashville: Thomas Nelson, 1998.

Nash, Ronald H. *Christian Faith and Historical Understanding.* Dallas: Probe, 1984.

Schmidt, Alvin J. and Paul Maier. *Under the Influence: How Christianity Transformed Civilization.* Grand Rapids, Mich.: Zondervan: 2001

ENDNOTES

1. W.F. Albright, "Toward a More Conservative View," *Christianity Today,* Jan. 18, 1963, p. 4.

2. H.G. Wells, *The Outline of History* (Garden City, N.Y.: Garden City Publishing, 1921), p. 497.

3. Gleason L. Archer, Jr., *A Survey of Old Testament Introduction* (Chicago: Moody Press, 1968), p. 19.

4. Nelson Glueck, *Biblical Archaeologist,* vol. 22 (Dec. 1959), p. 101.

5. John Warwick Montgomery, *Human Rights and Human Dignity* (Dallas, Tex.: Probe Books, 1986), p. 137.

6. Cornelius Tacitus, *Annals XV.* 44; cited in McDowell, *Evidence that Demands a Verdict,* p. 84.

7. Bruce M. Metzger, *The New Testament: Its Background, Growth, and Content* (Nashville: Abingdon Press, 1965), p. 78.

8. D.W. Bebbington, *Patterns in History* (Downers Grove, Ill.: InterVarsity Press, 1979), p. 169.

9. Herbert Butterfield, *Christianity and History* (New York: Charles Scribner's Sons, 1950), p. 66.

10. C. S. Lewis, *Miracles: A Preliminary Study* (London: Geoffrey Bles, 1952), p. 149. Norman Geisler describes Lewis' work on miracles, as "The best overall apologetic for miracles written in this century;" *Miracles and Modern Thought,* p. 167.

11. *God, History, and Historians,* ed. C.T. McIntire, (New York: Oxford University Press, 1977), p. 201.

12. John Warwick Montgomery, *The Shape of the Past* (Minneapolis: Bethany Fellowship, 1975), p. 42.

CHAPTER 12

Worldviews in Conflict

KEY QUESTION

Why should Christians understand
other worldviews?

KEY IDEAS

Believers must not only ground their
philosophy in Christ but also must know how
to respond to the arguments of other worldviews by offering better arguments.

KEY QUOTE

"We demolish arguments and every pretension
that sets itself up against the knowledge of God,
and we take captive every thought to make it
obedient to Christ."

—The Apostle Paul

SUMMARY

The biblical Christian worldview was the nursery of Western civilization and the foundation of the American experiment in ordered liberty. Yet today, Christianity is in retreat in almost every area of our society. This retreat began over 150 years ago when the great revivals that swept the country focused on the emotions and not the mind. Later, in the early 1900's, the church found itself unprepared to face the intellectual challenges of liberal theology and withdrew further into its shell, shielding itself from the primary shapers of culture—education, politics, and the media. Because of the void left by the church's retreat, people of a different worldview stepped in to champion their own brands of truth.

The effect of loss of a Christian influence has been predictable—an increasingly dark and tasteless society. Yet Christ directed His followers to provide a "salt and light" influence on society (Matthew 5:13-14). This means getting outside the confines of the church building and taking an active part in the social, political, and intellectual life of our communities. In order to have this kind of influence, Christians must gain an understanding of the times in which we live which means, at a minimum, discerning the competing worldviews that vie for our souls and the future of civilization. This entails understanding the Secular Humanist, Marxist/Leninist, and Cosmic Humanist worldviews.

In Acts 17, the Apostle Paul presented the gospel to people who held to a different worldview because he understood something about their philosophy and used that knowledge to his advantage. He carefully observed the religious expression of the Athenians as evidenced by their many statues of gods and goddesses throughout the city. Finding a point of common ground in their religious worldview, Paul moved to the biblical truth of God's judgment and the Good News of Christ's resurrection.

The Worldviews in Focus curriculum is based on the belief that by learning to contrast worldviews, students improve their overall conceptual skills. While this text presents a case for a biblical worldview, it is important for Christians to know something about other world-views that compete for their hearts and minds. This chapter gives a brief overview of three important worldviews that every Christian should understand.

But first, we must respond to a common objection. Some people feel that Christians should be shielded from non-Christian views. Some even use as an example how FBI agents are trained to identify counterfeit money by looking only at real bills, implying that Christians should study only the Bible and not waste time or

The ability to identify counterfeits—whether money or philosophies—requires knowing what "the real thing" as well as the fake looks like.

energy learning about "counterfeit" religions. But the problem with using this illustration is that it is based on false information. FBI training does include examining fake bills! In a similar way, studying a biblical perspective alone is not enough to prepare Christians to face other worldviews, especially those taught on the university campuses of today and presented through the mass media—movies, music, and news reporting.

We agree with Paul's admonition in Colossians 2:8 and 2 Corinthians 10:3-5, that a believer must not only ground his philosophy on Christ, but also must know how to "demolish" the arguments of other worldviews with better arguments. We do this best when we recognize the deceptions inherent in other worldviews. As Paul faced the religious humanists of his day in Acts 17, so the faithful and aware Christian must face the religious humanists of our day. In the West this means facing the Secular, Marxist, and Cosmic varieties.

THE MARXIST/LENINIST WORLDVIEW

Marxism/Leninism is a well-developed, atheistic worldview. Marxist/Leninists have developed a perspective regarding each of the ten disciplines—usually in great detail. Often, Marxism produces a "champion" of its perspective in the various fields (for example, I. P. Pavlov in psychology or T. D. Lysenko in biology). This alone makes Marxism worthy of study, but the main reason it is crucial for Christians to understand Marxism is that Marxism is one of Christianity's most vocal detractors.

This fact becomes all the more sinister when one realizes that some Christian groups have attempted to combine their Christianity with Marxism. Evangelical voices often referred to as the "Christian Left" have been known to support the Marxist position. The World Council of Churches saw no inconsistency in holding its meetings behind the Iron Curtain before it disintegrated.

The liberal American churches' position regarding Marxism does not, of course, take into account the profound incompatibility of their faith with the Marxist worldview.

The destruction of the Berlin wall epitomizes the failure of communism in practice, but many intellectuals—especially in America—continue to give credence to communist philosophy.

Some might raise the objection that the Marxist/Leninist worldview has already been proved to be a failure and completely incompatible with reality, as witnessed by the downfall of communist countries all over the world. Why, in light of these events, does one need to study the Marxist/Leninist perspective? Isn't Marxist ideology dead?

There are two answers to that question. First, while Marxism has crumbled in many countries, it still holds others in its death grip—Cuba and China, for example, and some African and Latin American countries (under the guise of Liberation Theology). If even one country is held captive by Marxism, people somewhere are suffering. Marxism/Leninism hates resistance, and will crush believers in rival worldviews any way necessary, even with tanks.

The second reason is that neo-Marxism is— incredibly!—the dominant perspective being taught on many American university campuses. In an article titled "Marxism in U.S. Classrooms,"

10,000 Marxist professors on U.S. campuses

U.S. News and World Report notes that there are ten thousand Marxist professors on America's campuses.[1] Georgie Anne Geyer says, that "the percentage of Marxist faculty numbers can range from an estimated 90 percent in some midwestern universities."[2] Arnold Beichman says that "Marxist academics are today's power elite in the universities."[3]

"The strides made by Marxism at American universities in the last two decades are breathtaking," says New York University's Herbert London. "Every discipline has been affected by its preachment, and almost every faculty now counts among its members a resident Marxist scholar."[4] The Marxist influence has reached its most alarming heights in the humanities departments of American universities. "With a few notable exceptions," says former Yale professor Roger Kimball, "our most prestigious liberal arts colleges and universities have installed the entire radical menu at the center of their humanities curriculum at both the undergraduate and the graduate level."[5] The result of this neo-Marxist influence has been that the culture wars are sometimes the fiercest on campuses across America, with battles being waged over political correctness, multiculturalism, deconstructionism, and postmodernism.

The Marxist worldview is alive and well in the American classroom. As Dr. Fred Schwarz says, "The colleges and universities are the nurseries of communism."[6] Christian students must not get caught up in these nurseries.

THE SECULAR HUMANIST WORLDVIEW

Marxism, however, is not the only worldview that threatens to take the classroom hostage. Secular Humanism also vies for control of education.

In fact, Secular Humanism, is the dominant worldview in our secular colleges and universities. It has even made gains in many Christian colleges and universities!

John Dewey, a signer of the *Humanist Manifesto*, has been a major influence in American public education during the past 100 years.

Christians considering a college education must be well versed in the humanistic worldview or risk losing their own Christian perspective by default. Why? Because humanist professors are unwilling to present the Christian perspective accurately, while many Christian educators feel duty-bound to give fair representation to the humanist viewpoint.

Humanists recognize the classroom as a powerful context for indoctrination. They understand that many worldviews exist and they believe humanists must use the classroom to flush out "unenlightened" worldviews and encourage individuals to embrace their worldview. Christianity has been deliberately—some would say brilliantly—erased from America's educational system. The direction of America's education can be seen as a descent from Jonathan Edwards (1750) and the Christian influence, through Horace Mann (1842) and the Unitarian influence, to John Dewey (1933) and the humanist influence.

But we contend that Jonathan Edwards has more to say than John Dewey, and that Christianity should get back into the public square and influence educational policy. The Christian worldview is a fitting competitor to Dewey's religious view. Hosea's statement, "My people are destroyed for lack of knowledge" (4:6), applies in spades to Christian college-bound students. Surveys of Christians in college reveal that many never recover from their educational befuddlement, lapsing instead into atheism, materialism, new morality, evolutionism, or globalism. Studies reveal that on some campuses, up to 51 percent of the Christian freshmen "drop-out" of the "born again" category by their senior year![7] Others suffer for years from their near loss of faith. Those who are well prepared, however, survive and flourish. If you want more information about how to prepare for college, read Appendix C, "Just for Parents."

America's colleges and universities are not the only areas of Secular Humanist influence, however. The mass media continually publish and broadcast the humanist worldview. The 1990 "Humanist of the Year" was Ted Turner, founder of CNN and former chief executive officer of Turner Broadcasting System. In 1985 Turner founded the Better World Society, and presently, he is offering $500,000 to anyone able to invent a new worldview suitable for the new,

peaceful earth. According to Turner, "Christianity is a religion for losers," and Christ should not have bothered dying on the cross.

Still another reason for examining the humanist worldview is that, besides Ted Turner, many humanists have gained positions of considerable influence in our society. B.F. Skinner, Abraham Maslow, Carl Rogers, and Erich Fromm, all former "Humanists of the Year," have powerfully affected psychology. Carl Sagan, another "Humanist of the Year," preached his humanism on a widely heralded television series, Cosmos. Norman Lear has produced and otherwise influenced a number of the shows on television today. Ethical decisions are made for our young people by "Humanist of the Year" Faye Wattleton, former director of Planned Parenthood. Humanist Isaac Asimov wrote tirelessly for his cause. Clearly, humanists are willing to support their worldview—often more faithfully than Christians.

THE COSMIC HUMANIST WORLDVIEW

In recent years, a fourth worldview has gained visibility across the United States, one we have labeled "Cosmic Humanism." Cosmic Humanism is the broad heading for an ideology consisting of a mixture of neo-paganism, or Wicca, and neo-pantheism, better known as the New Age Movement (NAM). Because it professes a marked disdain for dogma, this worldview is more vaguely defined than the other three. Indeed, some Cosmic Humanists go so far as to claim that their worldview "has no religious doctrine or teachings of its own."[8]

> *"The New Age is the ultimate eclectic religion of self: Whatever you decide is right for you is what's right."*
> —JOHANNA MICHAELSEN

This attitude, according to most New Agers, results from the belief that truth resides within each individual and, therefore, no one can claim a corner on the truth or dictate truth to another. "The New Age," explains Christian writer Johanna Michaelsen, "is the ultimate eclectic religion of self: Whatever you decide is right for you is what's right, as long as you don't get narrow-minded and exclusive about it."[9]

By assuming that truth resides within each individual, however, one lays the cornerstone for a worldview. Granting oneself the power to discern all truth is a facet of theology, and this theology has ramifications that many Cosmic Humanists have already discovered. Some have begun, grudgingly, to consider their movement a worldview. Marilyn Ferguson, author of *The Aquarian Conspiracy* (a book referred to as "the New Age watershed classic"), says the movement ushers in a "new mind—the ascendance of a startling worldview."[10] This worldview is summed up in its skeletal form, agreeable to virtually every Cosmic Humanist, by Jonathan Adolph: "In its broadest sense, New Age thinking can be characterized as a form of utopianism, the desire to create a better society, a 'New Age' in which humanity lives in harmony with itself, nature, and the cosmos."[11]

While the New Age movement still appears to be fragmented and without focused leadership, it has grown at a remarkable rate. The Stanford Research Institute estimates that "the number of New Agers in America could be as high as 5 to 10 percent of the population—12 million or more people."[12] Others have put the figure as high as 60 million, although this includes people who merely believe in reincarnation and astrology. John Randolph Price, a world leader of the New Age movement, says, "there are more than half a billion New Age advocates on the planet at this time, working among various religious groups."[13]

Further, people adhering to the Cosmic Humanist worldview are gaining power in our society and around the world. Malachi Martin lists dozens of organizations that are either New Age or sympathetic to New Age thinking. Barbara Marx Hubbard, a spokeswoman for the New Age, made a bid for the 1984 Democratic vice presidential nomination. In addition, Wicca is gaining new adherents. As Craig S. Hawkins writes:

> **A threatening storm is brewing on the religious horizon: the winds of occultism are blowing ever more strongly across the land. In the past two to three decades, America and much of Western Europe have seen a resurgence of paganism and witchcraft. Paganism is attempting a resurrection from the dead, a revival of the old gods and goddesses of pre-Christian polytheistic nature religions and mystery cults (e.g., Celtic, Norse, Greek, Egyptian, Roman, and other traditions of the Western world).[14]**

Many come to Wicca after reading *The Spiral Dance: A Rebirth of the Ancient Religion of the Great Goddess* (1979), a best-selling introduction to Wiccan teachings and rituals written by Starhawk (née Miriam Simos), a witch from California. Other young people are being drawn to consider this worldview through books and films like *Harry Potter*,[15] or by the influence of popular neo-pagan oriented television shows such as *Charmed* or *Buffy the Vampire Slayer*. Some estimate there may be more than 750,000 adherents of Wicca and related neo-pagan faiths in the United States.[16] Clearly, Cosmic Humanism is becoming a "fourth force" in the Western hemisphere.

A CALL TO DEDICATION

The acceptance of many of these distortions of the truth by the Christian community is our greatest shame. Countless Christians, thanks to books like *Biology Through the Eyes of Faith*, have accepted evolutionary theory, many so firmly that they treat creationists as unwelcome brethren or worse. Many Christian colleges that have finally recognized the scientific weaknesses of theistic Darwinian evolution still shun special creationism, moving instead toward punctuated equilibrium. Other Christians are embracing various forms of Marxism and socialism, calling it "Liberation Theology." Some have bought into concepts like self-actualization, behaviorism, feminism, pro-choice, Eastern meditation, and world government.

Why do Christians so easily accept inconsistencies in their worldview? It is our position that too many ignore Paul's admonition that they not be taken captive "through vain and deceitful philosophy" (Colossians 2:8). With respect to avoiding inconsistencies, non-Christians are much more consistent. There are no Marxist/ Leninist creationists. There are no New Agers who believe in ethical absolutes. Christians, who trust the Scriptures and therefore have access to the one worldview based on eternal truth, should be the first to recognize the bankruptcy of secular religious views. Yet, all too often, they are the first to embrace them!

> *"The humanistic system of values has now become the predominant way of thinking in most of the power centers of society."*
> —JAMES C. DOBSON AND GARY L. BAUER

Obviously, the job of training Christian thinkers is not being done very well. The Christian worldview is in retreat in nearly every arena of American life—

including our universities, media, arts, music, law, business, medicine, psychology, sociology, public schools, and government. "The humanistic system of values has now become the predominant way of thinking in most of the power centers of society,"[17] claim James C. Dobson and Gary L. Bauer. According to Dobson and Bauer, the Christian worldview has only two power centers remaining in America—the church and the family—and both of them are under tremendous pressure to surrender.

There is compelling evidence that our popular secularized culture is having a greater influence than either the Christian home or the church. The Nehemiah Institute surveyed Christian teenagers attending evangelical churches across the U.S. and found that, in answering questions dealing with each of the ten disciplines, these young people respond no differently than their Secular Humanist counterparts! And when it comes to the major political, social, economic, religious, and educational issues of our day, the results over the past twelve years demonstrate a definite trend away from biblical Christianity and toward Marxist socialism.[18] These results point to the disturbing fact that we are losing the culture war among Christian youth, but truth is our greatest weapon.

> The Christian worldview has only two power centers remaining in America—the church and the family —and both of them are under tremendous pressure to surrender.

WHAT ARE WE TO DO?

- Go on the offensive! Light a candle (Matthew 5:14).
- Pray (2 Chronicles 7:14; Colossians 1:9-14).
- Study (2 Timothy 2:15).
- Understand the times (1 Chronicles 12:32).
- Rebuild the foundations (Psalm 11:3).
- Spread the word with courage and conviction (Hebrews 11; 1 Peter 3:15-16).

(For helpful sources, see Appendix D.)

One of America's great Christian statesmen, Theodore Roosevelt, looked upon the Christian worldview as a comprehensive frame of reference touching the totality of life. For him, Christianity was not just a plan of salvation, an ethical system, an exercise in mysticism for an hour or two a week, but truth. It

Theodore Roosevelt, president of the United States from 1901 to 1909, saw the Christian worldview as a comprehensive frame of reference for all of life.

was truth about all things, for all men, for all times.[19]

Philosophy students at Charles University in Prague, Czechoslovakia, told their professors they had had enough of Marxist/Leninist dialectics. American students can do the same—casting Secular, Marxist and Cosmic Humanism out of the classroom. But such a stand will not come easy; it will take a rebirth of morality, a revival of spiritual interests, a renewal of intellectual honesty, and a recovery of courage. It will take a shoring up of the family and a reawakening in our churches. It will take concentrated effort to re-establish the influence of Christianity on our culture, but it can be done.

To accomplish this, Christians must shore up their worldview and teach it to young and old alike. We must immerse ourselves in Christian theology, Christian philosophy, Christian ethics, Christian politics, Christian economics, Christian psychology, Christian sociology, Christian biology, Christian law, and Christian history.

Some progress has been made in this direction. Leading the way are men like Chuck Colson who, through his writings and popular daily radio commentary, *Breakpoint,* challenge the Christian community to apply a biblical worldview in the public arena. Christian philosophers like Alvin Plantinga, J.P. Moreland, William Lane Craig, and Norman Geisler have gone to great lengths to defend Christianity from its Secular Humanist opponents through seminars, debates, and books.

Henry Morris, Duane Gish, Ken Cummings, A.E. Wilder-Smith, and a host of Christian men of science have demonstrated the veracity of the creationist position. Wendell Bird's *Origin of Species Revisited* contains enough scientific data to sink evolutionary theory. Thaxton, Bradley and Olson's *The Mystery of Life's Origins* and Davis and Kenyon's *Of Pandas and People* encourage the position that science and Christianity are allies.

D. James Kennedy in *What if Jesus Had Never Been Born?* and *What if the Bible Had Never Been Written?*, along with Alvin J. Schmidt in *Under the Influence,* demonstrate beyond a shadow of a doubt how Christianity has transformed civilization

> **Nearly everything good about Western Civilization has its origin in Jesus Christ and His followers.**

through the centuries. Nearly everything good about Western Civilization has its origin in Jesus Christ and His followers. This is certainly what *Newsweek* (March 29, 1999) had in mind when it said, "By any secular standard, Jesus is also the dominant figure of Western culture." The article mentions art, science, society, politics, economics, marriage, family, ethics, body, and soul—"all have been touched and often radically transformed by Christian influence."

Still, much more needs to be accomplished to remind the world of the truth of Christianity and give encouragement for the future. We need Christian young people, strong in the faith, to follow Cal Thomas, Britt Hume, Tony Snow, Ann Coulter, and Fred Barnes into the media, to take charge of the universities, to run for Congress and school boards, and to espouse Christian sociology (with a strong

> *"By any secular standard, Jesus is also the dominant figure of Western culture."*
> —*NEWSWEEK* MAGAZINE

emphasis on traditional family values). We need Christian artists challenging us with something that feeds the spirit and fuels the imagination, instead of art, literature, and music fit for the cultural sewer.

> **Christians can reclaim law, history, politics, economics, and all other disciplines.**

Christians can reclaim law, history, politics, economics, and all other disciplines. Understanding themselves to be men and women created to serve God, they can heed the call to excellence more profoundly than proponents of any other worldview.

CONCLUSION

After working our way through a systematic analysis of the ten major components of a worldview, our studied conclusions are that:

- In *theology,* the evidence for the existence of a personal and holy God, a designed universe, and an earth prepared for human life far outweighs any argument for atheism or pantheism.

- In *philosophy,* the notion that mind (logos) precedes matter is far superior to the atheistic stance of matter preceding mind.

- In *biology,* the concept of a living God who creates life fits the evidence better than any notion of spontaneous generation and evolution.

- In *psychology,* understanding people as inherently sinful beings in need of a Savior far outweighs thinking of them as inherently perfectible and guilt-free.

- In *ethics,* the concept that right and wrong are absolutes based on the nature and character of a personal, loving, just God is far superior both theoretically and practically to any concept of moral relativism.

- In *sociology,* the biblical family of father, mother, and child transcends any experiments in trial marriages, homosexuality, and the like.

- In *law,* the notion that God hates the perversion of justice is far superior to any theory of legal relativism or positive law.

- In *politics,* the Christian belief that human rights are a gift from God protected by government is more logically persuasive, morally appealing, and politically sound than any atheistic theory that maintains human rights are a largess of the state.

- In *economics,* the concept of stewardship of private property and using resources responsibly to glorify God is more noble than the notion of a society in which common ownership destroys individual responsibility and work incentives.

- In *history,* the veracity of the Bible and its promise of a future kingdom ushered in by Jesus Christ is far more credible than vague, utopian, global schemes dreamed up by sinful, mortal human beings.

Indeed, we cannot imagine one category in which the non-Christian world-views outshine the Christian position. For example, putting Christian economics into practice results in prosperity and the reduction of poverty, while all forms of socialism (including the welfare state) guarantee various levels of poverty. God is indeed smarter than Plato and Marx. Putting Christian sociology into practice results in strong families that discourage societal trends toward drug use, crime, unemployment, poverty, and disease,

> **All forms of socialism guarantee various levels of poverty.**

whereas non-Christian experimentation with the family unit (including Secular Humanism's self-proclaimed "important role in the sexual revolution") causes society to disintegrate. Putting Christian law into practice results in the Magna Charta and the U.S. Constitution, guaranteeing human rights as God-ordained, while the history of positive law—in France for two centuries, in the Soviet Union

> **In every discipline, the Christian worldview shines brighter than its competition.**

for seventy years, and in the U.S. for the last half-century—has been a history of blood baths. (Yes, blood baths in the United States: 1.5 million unborn babies killed every year by abortion.) Most importantly, of course, putting Christian theology and philosophy into practice results in salvation of the soul (Matthew 16:26), enlightenment of the mind, and purpose in living.

In other words, in every discipline, the Christian worldview shines brighter than its competition, is more realistic, better explains man and the universe, is true to the Bible, is more scientific, is more intellectually satisfying and defensible, and best of all, is in keeping with and faithful to the one person who has had the greatest influence in heaven and on earth—Jesus Christ. To be faithful to Christ

> *Matthew 16:26 What will it benefit a man if he gains the whole world yet loses his life? Or what will a man give in exchange for his life?*

entails, at the minimum, taking every idea captive for Christ (2 Corinthians 10:5) and not allowing humanistic worldviews to take us captive (Colossians 2:8).

The first and last words Christ Jesus spoke to Peter were, "Follow Me." He speaks those same words to us still.

RECOMMENDED READING FOR ADVANCED STUDY:
UNDERSTANDING WORLDVIEWS

Anderson, Martin. *Imposters in the Temple: American Intellectuals Are Destroying Our Universities and Cheating Our Students of Their Future.* New York: Simon & Schuster, 1992.

Bloom, Allan. *The Closing of the American Mind: How Higher Education Has Failed Democracy and Impoverished the Souls of Today's Students.* New York: Simon and Schuster, 1987.

Breese, Dave. *Seven Men Who Rule the World from the Grave.* Chicago: Moody Press, 1990.

Kimball, Roger. *Tenured Radicals.* New York: Harper & Row, 1990

LaHaye, Tim and David A. Noebel. *Mind Siege.* Dallas: Word Publishing, 2001.

Marsden, George. *The Soul of the American University: From Protestant Establishment to Established Nonbelief.* New York: Oxford University Press, 1994.

Nash, Ronald. *The Closing of the American Heart.* Brentwood, Tenn.: Wolgemuth & Hyatt, 1990.

Noebel, David A. *Understanding the Times: The Religious Worldviews of Our Day and the Search for Truth.* Eugene, Ore.: Harvest House Publishers, 1991.

Sowell, Thomas. *Inside American Education: The Decline, the Deception, the Dogmas.* New York: MacMillan, 1993.

ENDNOTES

1. David B. Richardson, "Marxism in U.S. Classrooms," *U.S. News and World Report,* January 25, 1982, pp. 42-5.

2. Georgie Anne Geyer, "Marxism Thrives on Campus," *The Denver Post,* August 29, 1989, p. B7.

3. Ibid.

4. Herbert London, "Marxism Thriving on American Campuses," *The World and I,* January 1987, p. 189.

5. Roger Kimball, *Tenured Radicals* (New York: Harper & Row, 1990), p. xiii. Christian young people should read Kimball's book, then Allan Bloom's *The Closing of the American Mind: How Higher Education has Failed Democracy and Impoverished the Souls of Today's Students* (New York: Simon and Schuster, 1987), and finally Ronald Nash's *The Closing of the American*

Heart (Brentwood Tenn.: Wolgemuth & Hyatt, 1990) to grasp what Christian students face in America's colleges and universities.

6. "Newsletter of the Christian Anti-Communist Crusade," P.O. Box 890, Long Beach, Ca. 90801; February 1, 1988.

7. Gary Lyle Railsback, "An Exploratory Study of the Religiosity and Related Outcomes Among College Students," Doctoral dissertation, University of California at Los Angeles, 1994.

8. Jonathan Adolph, "What Is New Age?" *New Age Journal,* Winter 1988, p. 11.

9. Johanna Michaelsen, *Like Lambs to the Slaughter* (Eugene, Ore.: Harvest House, 1989), p. 11.

10. Marilyn Ferguson, *The Aquarian Conspiracy* (Los Angeles: J. P. Tarcher, Inc., 1980), p. 23.

11. Adolph, "What is New Age?" p. 6.

12. Ray A. Yungen, *For Many Shall Come in My Name,* (Salem, Oregon: Ray Yungen, 1989), p. 34.

13. John Randolph Price, *The Superbeings* (Austin, Tex.: Quartus Books, 1981), pp. 51.

14. Craig S. Hawkins, "The Modern World of Witchcraft," *The Christian Research Journal,* Winter/Spring 1990, page 8.

15. See "Harry Potter: Witchcraft Repacked," Jeremiah Films, P.O. Box 1710, Hemet, CA, 92546. 1-800-828-2290.

16. It is difficult to estimate the number of Wiccans and neo-pagans because of the nature of their religious belief and practice, not being prone to organizing beyond small groups of local adherents who usually do not advertise their existence. Estimates of their numbers in the U.S. vary, but range from 5,000 to 5 million according to the Religious Tolerance website:

    www.religioustolerance.org/wic_nbr.htm

17. James C. Dobson and Gary L. Bauer, *Children at Risk: The Battle For the Hearts and Minds of Our Kids* (Dallas, Tex.: Word, 1990), p. 22.

18. The Nehemiah Institute estimates that if evangelical students continue the same downward pattern they have exhibited based on survey scores over the past 13 years, the majority of Christian teenagers will be hard-core Secular Humanists/Marxists by the year 2014. For information about the "P.E.E.R.S." survey from the Nehemiah Institute, write them at 1323 No. 3rd St., Aberdeen, SD, 57401, call 1-800-948-3101, or visit their website at www.nehemiahinstitute.com.

19. George Grant, *Carry a Big Stick* (Elkton, MD; Highland Books, 1996), p. 169.

APPENDIX A: FOUR WESTERN WORLDVIEW MODELS

	BIBLICAL CHRISTIANITY	SECULAR HUMANISM	MARXISM / LENINISM	COSMIC HUMANISM
SOURCES	THE BIBLE	HUMANIST MANIFESTOS I, II, III	WRITINGS OF MARX AND LENIN	WRITINGS OF SPANGLER, FERGUSON, ETC.
THEOLOGY	Theism	Atheism	Atheism	Pantheism
PHILOSOPHY	Supernaturalism	Naturalism	Dialectical Materialism	Non-Naturalism
BIOLOGY	Creation	Darwinian Evolution	Punctuated Evolution	Cosmic Evolution
PSYCHOLOGY	Image of God / Fallen	Self-Actualization	Behaviorism	Higher Consciousness
ETHICS	Ethical Absolutes	Ethical Relativism	Proletariat Morality	Individual Autonomy
SOCIOLOGY	Traditional Home, Church and State	Non-Traditional Family	Abolition of Home, Church and State	Non-Traditional Home, Church and State
LAW	Biblical and Natural Law	Positive Law	Proletariat Law	Self-Law
POLITICS	Justice/Freedom/Order	World Government	New World Order	New Age Order
ECONOMICS	Stewardship of Property	Socialism	Socialism / Communism	Universal Enlightened Production
HISTORY	Resurrection	Historical Evolution	Historical Materialism	Evolutionary Godhood

APPENDIX B: GOD'S CREATIVE AND REDEMPTIVE ORDER

CATEGORY	CREATIVE ORDER (God's creative activity in the world)		REDEMPTIVE ORDER (Christ's role in the world)	
THEOLOGY	Gen. 1:1	God is!	Col. 2:9	Christ is Fullness of the Godhead
PHILOSOPHY	Gen. 1:1	1) Time 2) Creation 3) Heaven 4) Earth	Jn. 1:1 Col. 2:3	"Logos" = Wisdom & knowledge
BIOLOGY	Gen. 1:21	Created "Kinds"	John 1:4	Christ is "Life"
PSYCHOLOGY	Gen. 2:7	Man is a living soul	Luke 1:46-47	Savior of the soul
ETHICS	Gen. 2:9	Good / Evil	John 1:9	Christ is "Light"
SOCIOLOGY	Gen. 1:28	Family = Fruitfulness	Luke 1:30-31	Son of Mary
LAW	Gen. 3:11	Command	Gen. 49:10	Scepter of Judah
POLITICS	Gen. 9:6	Shedding blood	Rev. 19:16	King of kings Lord of lords
ECONOMICS	Gen. 1:29	Food = basic economic principle	Psalm 50:10-12	Christ is Owner
HISTORY	Gen. 3:15	Seed of woman Seed of serpent	Rev. 22:13	Alpha & Omega

APPENDIX C
Just For Parents

(This appendix is an excerpt from Summit Ministries' Guide to Choosing a College *by Dr. Ronald Nash and Jeff Baldwin.)*

Suppose you won the lottery. Suppose a millionaire found your name in the phone book and designated you as his sole heir. Suppose you could wallpaper your home with $100 bills, and still have money to burn. Would you be willing to take a $75,000 gamble? Would you be willing to gamble $75,000 *and* your son's or daughter's future?

Most parents don't have $75,000 to throw around, nor are they willing to risk their children's future on a bad bet. Until college. Then, for whatever reason, families will spend $75,000 (or more!) on an "education" that does their children more harm than good. Christian parents who wouldn't let their kids out of the house without a compass and a flare gun suddenly pay good money to see their kids indoctrinated by anti-Christian professors.

Let's face it: sending your kids to college is a big investment, both financially and spiritually. Before making *any* decisions, you should set some ground rules and prepare to help your children in any and every way.

A QUESTION OF VALUES

Whenever we choose thoughtfully, we rank things according to their importance to us and choose those options that offer more of the things that matter most to us. There are a number of beliefs that should be important to all who are Christians in the New Testament sense of the word. But some Christians also get excited about less central—or more debatable—issues. Some of us are Calvinists, while others are Arminians. Some are Pentecostal or charismatic. Some are dispensationalist. When families feel strongly about these matters, they might decide to avoid a college where such a belief is treated unsympathetically. And when a Methodist or Calvinistic or charismatic family finds themselves leaning toward a college that they know will treat their convictions sympathetically, their action is both understandable and proper.

LEVELS OF PARENTAL CONCERN

Parental concern for children functions on several different levels. Where parents stand on this ladder of concern will affect the quality of their influence on their college decision-making process.

1. EMOTIONAL CONCERN

The first and most basic level of parental concern is emotional. This is most likely where all parents begin. We love our children; we care what happens to them; we want the best for them. There is nothing wrong with this level of parental concern for one's children. The problem arises when parents' concern for their children fails to go beyond this level. Your concern for them must function on other levels as well.

2. SPIRITUAL CONCERN

Many parents fail to see beyond the goal of temporal happiness and success for their children—usually linked to "a good job" that includes a salary that will permit them to satisfy their material wants and needs. For such parents, a college education is simply a means to this end. Wise parents recognize that there is more to life than this. God calls His children to live their lives for Him and others. Parents at the level of spiritual concern want more than earthly success and material prosperity for their children. They want their children to be faithful believers who sincerely want to do the Lord's will. The level of spiritual concern involves conversion, Christian living, and Christian service. The notion of Christian service should be seen in the context of what Martin Luther called the doctrine of Christian vocation. God does not call every Christian into full-time Christian work or ministry. We should thank God for talented young people who pursue a career in ministry. But, we should also thank God for faithful young people who fulfill their Christian vocations as farmers, teachers, business people, and auto mechanics.

3. THEOLOGICAL CONCERN

I have never met a genuine Christian who disparaged the importance of conversion, faith, commitment, sacrifice, Bible study, holy living, and the like. But I know lots of Christians who have not yet seen the importance of sound doctrine. It is important that we believe (spiritual concern), but it is also important *what* we believe (theological concern).

More than eighty years ago, a great Scottish theologian named James Orr puzzled over Christians who consider doctrine unimportant: "If there is a religion in the world which exalts the office of teaching, it is safe to say that it is the religion of Jesus Christ. This is precisely where Christianity distinguishes itself from other religions—it does contain doctrine. It comes to men with definite, positive teaching; it claims to be the truth; it bases religion on knowledge. . . . A religion based on mere feeling is the vaguest, most unreliable, most unstable of all things. A strong, stable, religious life can be built upon no other ground than that of intelligent conviction."

Your children must know the objective dimension of their faith, to understand what they, as Christians, are supposed to believe. They should know the sound reasons why Christians believe these truths. The children of many Christian parents enter college with no preparation for the challenges to their faith. Suddenly, they are confronted by a professor who tells them about "the problem of evil." Without any guidance or help, some of these students begin to think that maybe God isn't all-powerful after all; or perhaps God doesn't really exist. All too often, if they ask their parents about these problems, their parents don't have any answers either. Parents who fail to rise to the level of theological concern cannot provide help for their children in these matters. So, the first step in getting children theologically prepared for what awaits them is for parents of those children to prepare themselves. I believe this task is every bit as important as finding the money to pay for your children's education.

4. INTELLECTUAL CONCERN

What often makes this last level so tough to achieve is its apparent lack of relevance to typical religious concerns. Gaining knowledge for its own sake—the study of history or mathematics or economics or philosophy or art or music—seems pointless to some when no direct relationship to Christianity is apparent. But consider that the first and greatest commandment, according to Jesus, requires us to love God with all our heart and all our soul and all our mind (see Matthew 22:37). The practice of compartmentalizing knowledge into sacred and secular is unbiblical and leads to the dangerous notion that secular knowledge is somehow less important, more worldly, and hence, unfit, for the spiritual Christian. However, the truth we can find outside the Bible is important and worthy of careful study. Even revealed truth requires study and interpretation, tasks that can be aided by an education in such "secular" subjects as philosophy and history.

In 1987 and 1988, a serious book by University of Chicago philosopher, Allan Bloom, became a best-seller. *The Closing of the American Mind* is worthwhile reading for any Christian who aspires to the intellectual level of concern. While his is not a religious book, much that Bloom says about higher education will be appreciated by Christian readers. Bloom writes that many families "have nothing to give their children in the way of a vision of the world, . . . The family requires a certain authority and wisdom about the ways of the heavens and of men. The parents must have knowledge of what has happened in the past, and prescriptions for what ought to be, in order to resist the philistinism or the wickedness of the present." In other words, parents can help their children only when they themselves have acquired a foundation in certain important areas.

Bloom continues: "People sup together, play together, travel together, but they do not think together. Hardly any homes have any intellectual life whatsoever, let alone one that informs the vital interests of life." When was the last time your family spent time thinking together? Christians need to work at developing a Christian mind, and they should do this in partnership with other members of their family.

HELPING CHILDREN GET AN EARLY START

Every year, I teach an Introduction to Philosophy course to about 200 students, and I have begun to realize that many college students cannot write decent essays: The reason is that they simply have not read enough. They cannot spell because they haven't seen the words in print; they cannot write sentences because the little they learned about grammar hasn't been reinforced by reading;

their paragraphs do not rise above the mundane because their exposure to the vocabulary and writing style of good authors is limited. And so my first recommendation is to encourage your children to read. Allan Bloom points out that students "have lost the practice of and the taste for reading. They have not learned how to read, nor do they have the expectation of delight or improvement from reading." The failure to read good books, Bloom continues, "enfeebles the vision and strengthens our most fatal tendency—the belief that the here and now is all there is."

Children should be encouraged to read quality books suited to their ability. Ideally, at least one parent will read the book at the same time to discuss it with the child. In addition to classics, children should do the kind of reading and thinking that will prepare them to develop theologically. C.S. Lewis is a marvelous resource for this. His children's stories are an especially good way to get children to think about theological subjects, as well as to get them interested in Lewis as a writer. Any good reading program must include the Bible. Make sure a reliable, readable, version of the Bible is available. Along with providing spiritual direction, the Bible is important for understanding many literary classics. Encourage your children to read books that explain what Christians believe and why they believe this way. One such book is Paul Little's *Know Why You Believe.*

Consider ways of working an educational angle into your family travels. For families that can afford it, foreign travel frequently gets young people excited about new areas of study. My own children, for instance, became interested in learning the history of Great Britain after visiting England. A brief stop at the home of the Bronte sisters generated an desire to read their novels. A two-day stop in Edinburgh, Scotland, encouraged them to learn more about John Knox and the Scottish Reformation.

Your child's progress in high school should be carefully monitored. Watch her progress in writing courses. Be certain he takes the college preparatory program and skips none of the important courses in English, math, and history. Sometime before your child's junior year in high school, he or she should prepare for the college boards. Most good bookstores carry books that can help students get ready for the SAT and ACT tests.

For further reading about preparing children for college, you may want to secure a copy of the complete book from which this summary is taken: *Summit Ministries' Guide to Choosing A College.*

APPENDIX D

Resources for Keeping Up with the Times

We recommend that you subscribe to a conservative or Christian publication in order to gain a balanced perspective on current issues. You may try one or more of the resources noted below. While we do not endorse everything that is printed in these publications, they generally give a conservative, biblically oriented perspective.

The Journal: A monthly publication from Summit Ministries, edited by David A. Noebel. It includes excerpts from books dealing with all ten disciplines covered in this text and representing all five worldviews: Biblical, Secular Humanist, Marxist/Leninist, Cosmic Humanist, and Postmodern. Although subscriptions to *The Journal* are free, Summit Ministries accepts donations to cover the cost of approximately $15 per year per subscription. Call (719) 685-9103. Or, receive the online edition and check archived issues on the Summit Ministries website at:

www.summit.org/Journal.htm.

World Magazine: A weekly news resource that covers state, national and worldwide issues in the news from a Christian perspective. $49.95/year. 800-951-6397. www.worldmag.com.

Breakpoint: A monthly commentary on faith and culture presented by Chuck Colson. An excellent, concise treatment of ideas from every area of study. $45.00/year. 800-457-6125. www.breakpoint.org.

Human Events: A conservative weekly newspaper with articles and commentaries on national and international news. It is a counter-balance to the liberal press' reporting on current issues. $50.00/year (introductory rate). 800-787-7557.

Citizen: The monthly magazine from Focus on the Family dealing with a variety of current issues related to Christian morality, government and the family. Suggested donation is $20.00/year. 800-232-6459.

Leadership University: An excellent website by Christian Leadership Ministries, the faculty ministry of Campus Crusade for Christ. It deals with current trends on university campuses and articles from Christian faculty ranging from the creation/evolution debate to the "politically correct" wars on campus. There are over 7,000 articles students can use to research papers or to defend their faith in class discussions. www.leaderu.com

Campus: Published three times a year, this conservative publication is written and edited by college students. Each issue describes current happenings on college campuses across America—everything from "Condom Week" to liberal professors to homosexual demands. No charge to students and faculty; all others $10.00/year. (800) 526-7022.

PHOTO CREDITS

Important Information about opening the Leader's Guide CD:

The files on the CD are in PDF format. In order to open the files, you must either already have Adobe® Acrobat® Reader on your system or you can install Adobe® Acrobat® Reader from the folder on your CD entitled "install." Simply insert the CD into your system and open the "install" folder and double-click the installer in that folder. Adobe® Acrobat® Reader is also available for download from the internet at:

http://www.adobe.com/products/acrobat/readstep2.html

Tips for Using the Leader's Guide CD:

The CD included in the back of this textbook features all of the support materials you will need to turn "Thinking Like a Christian" into a valuable and memorable learning experience for any group. There are four "tracks" of study available, depending on the context and maturity level of those you will be leading:

1. Homeschool. Support materials include lesson plans, teaching outlines, pupil handouts, recommended assignments, quizzes, and exams that allow you to present to your homeschool student a comprehensive course on worldview studies. This study provides extremely valuable perspective on other homeschool subjects such as history, science, philosophy, Bible, and economics.

2. High School Youth Group or Sunday School. Support materials include lesson plans, teaching outlines and pupil handouts that provide a high-energy experience to build a high schooler's confidence in his or her biblical worldview.

3. College Study Group or Sunday School. Support materials include lesson plans, teaching outlines, and pupil handouts that offer a compelling apologetic for the Christian worldview and enough background information to refute the opposing perspectives which every student will encounter during his or her college experience.

4. Adult Small Group Study or Sunday School. Support materials include lesson plans, teaching outlines, and pupil handouts to help adults handle the real-life issues that challenge the world view thinking of even a person of strong faith commitment.

As you open the CD, you will find a folder for each track. Within the folder for each track is a document called "Preliminaries" which details the components of that particular track. In addition, you will find that each lesson is in it's own folder. Within each of those folders, in turn, are the materials mentioned above that coincide with the information in each lesson.

For instance, suppose you were leading a youth group through a study of "Chapter 1—Thinking about Worldviews." First, open the CD folder for "Youth Group." Then, read the "Preliminaries" document. Then click on Lesson 1. There you will find the lesson plan, teaching outline and class handouts for Lesson 1. If you were to have the CD opened to this point, the organization would look something like this:

```
HOMESCHOOL
YOUTH GROUP
COLLEGE
ADULT
          PRELIMINARIES
          LESSON 1
                    Lesson Plan
                    Teaching Outline
                    Class Handouts
          LESSON 2
          LESSON 3
          (etc.)
```

Once you open the CD and get started, you'll find it quite user-friendly.

You may find the best way to use the teaching material is to print it out. By doing so, you will see how readily the components fit together. So, enjoy your teaching (and learning!).